THE

POSITION

A Framework for Financial Success

by Brandon Spiece and Dave Fleischer

Foreword by JL Collins

DEDICATIONS

DAVE FLEISCHER

I would like to dedicate this book to:

My parents - You raised me in a safe, caring and God-Centered household. There is no way I would be where I am today without you! The example you set living a frugal lifestyle laid the path for me to land safely upon arrival in the "real world." It is a pleasure to dedicate this book to you.

My sister - Kathy, it is rare to find people who shoot you straight! Your transparency about all things, and the in depth conversations that we've had over the years left a profound impact on my life.

My wife - Stephanie, you have such an inspirational, Godly heart of gold and I look forward to giving outrageously and traveling the world with you by my side. None of this would have occurred without your loving support! What an honor it is to "do life" with you.

My children - Before kids, I never believed I could have such unconditional love for another human being. Crosby and Elliot, it is a great pleasure to be your father. I am your biggest cheerleader and can't wait to see all that God has in store for you! Put God first in everything you do.

~Dave Fleischer

BRANDON SPIECE

I would like to dedicate this book to:

My parents, Glenn & Teresa - For your love and support over the years. You sacrificed so much so that my brothers and I could have opportunities that so many others don't have. You are the perfect example of what parents should be. I love you both very much.

My brothers, and their wives, Adam & Ashley and Ryan & Chandra - I am so proud of the families that you are raising. I pray that your children, my nieces and nephews, will live fulfilled, Christ-centered lives, build wealth, and give generously.

My fiancée, Lori Ann - Without you, this book would never have happened. Your love and faith inspire me to do things I would have never dreamed of doing before you came into my life. I love you with a love that is more than love.

My future bonus son, Patrick - You are an outstanding young man. I am excited for your future, and humbled by the fact that I get a front row seat to watch it unfold. The home that your mother and I share will always be your home.

~Brandon Spiece

DISCLAIMER

The information in this book reflects what Dave Fleischer and Brandon Spiece have learned about personal finances from their own experiences and from the experiences of those that they have talked with over the years. These lessons were confirmed by all of the guests that they have interviewed on *The Financially Independent Teacher's Podcast.*

The information in this book is for educational purposes only. This book is not a source of financial or legal advice. When it comes to your personal finances, no one can guarantee success. The publisher and authors of this book make no guarantee of financial results by using this book.

ACKNOWLEDGEMENTS

Dave and I would like to thank all of the guests that agreed to come on *The Financially Independent Teachers Podcast.* Your stories have inspired us and confirmed what we already thought was true: That teachers can build wealth and become financially independent.

We would also like to thank everyone that took the time to read the manuscript for this book at each stage of development. Your opinions and positive feedback encouraged us to keep going.

A special thank you to JL Collins for writing the Foreword. To have someone as accomplished as you come along and help a couple of eastern North Carolina Social Studies Teachers with a passion project speaks volumes about the kind of man you are. We will forever be grateful to you for investing in us.

FOREWORD

You've been lied to.

You've been told, as a teacher, you have no right to expect financial success. That financial independence (FI) is but a dream for the likes of you.

Or, even worse, you may not have ever even been introduced to the idea of FI. That there is such a thing. That it is a choice, a path, an option available to you. Yes, even as a teacher.

Indeed, *especially* as a teacher.

Here's something I'll bet you don't know. I didn't before reading this book.

Do you know what profession has produced the most net-worth millionaires in America? Well, (drum roll, please)...

... not teachers.

Cue trombone: Wah, wah, wah.

The gold and silver go to engineering and accounting.

But standing proud and strong right up there on the podium, in position #3 for the bronze, are teachers!

That's right. While the world at large has been telling you FI is for others, a whole bunch of your fellow teachers have basically said "screw that conventional wisdom, it's definitely for me." And off they went and did it.

This book is the result of countless conversations with these money savvy teachers, and it will tell you how they did it and how you can too.

As you'll see, along the way they learned not only is it possible, but as a teacher you are *perfectly positioned* to retire early and wealthy.

Bet you haven't heard that before. You might even be shaking your head in disbelief.

That's OK. I get it. After all, this runs counter to the conventional wisdom narrative you have been fed your entire life. Plus, it is good to be a skeptical, critical thinker who demands evidence. This is likely one of the skills with which you try hard to gift your students.

But so is nurturing an open and inquiring mind. So, before you close this book and walk away, give some thought to the idea that the world is filled with teachers who, possessed with the same opportunities, resources and, yes, limitations as you, have become free and wealthy.

For that possibility, this short read is certainly worth your time. The evidence is right here, and it is compelling.

You know teachers are smart, inquisitive, open to new ideas, hardworking, resourceful, and focused on making an impact in what they do. You are one. Achieving wealth is well within your abilities.

Although, to be clear, this isn't going to be easy. It's going to take effort and lean in close now so I can whisper this next part in your ear. It's the secret.

You are going to have to alter your way of thinking.

Not too many people can do this. It requires stepping away from the conventional wisdom that has made you so very comfortable, even as it has kept you poor.

This conventional wisdom is blind to that #3 podium position of wealth achievers' teachers have. It says you must accept teaching is a profession of poverty and sacrifice, undeserving of wealth.

It says you'll be expected to buy all the trinkets and trash needed to keep up with those Jones and have a "good life." It says you must embrace the utter nonsense that $800 car payments and credit card balances are normal.

And the silly notion such things are what earn you the respect and affection of your friends, and the love of your family.

This is where you'll need your critical thinking and skepticism most. If you can just step back for even a moment from these blinding lights for a clearer view, this all resolves into the obvious absurdity it really is.

Happiness and joy are not bought; with one exception:

When you use your money to buy your freedom and to own your time.

The FIT Position is filled with "truth bombs" that serve to bring this home. Want a taste? Here's one:

"Love grows best in small homes."

This is a book written by two teachers who have spent countless hours interviewing other teachers who have rejected the conventional and embraced the path to wealth.

These are the teachers who have torn apart that conventional wisdom and instead contributed to the growing #3 position. (Look out you engineers and accountants!)

In these pages they show you how it's done, how you can join them, and how being a teacher actually makes you uniquely suited to do it.

As the saying goes, when the student is ready, the teacher will appear. With this book and in these pages, you hold that teacher in your hands.

The question is, are you ready?

~JL Collins

CONTENTS

IMPERATIVE #1
BE FRUGAL

*"There is no dignity quite so impressive, and no one
independence quite so important,
as living within your means."*
~Calvin Coolidge

The book that you hold in your hands is the product of a passion project that Dave Fleischer started in the form of a podcast back in February of 2020. Dave was tired of hearing that teachers can't make it financially. He wanted to give teachers hope, and a path towards financial success. He had an idea to host a podcast whereby he could interview teachers that were doing well with money. He decided to recruit a co-host and that is where I come in. I was reluctant to join him. Not because I didn't believe in the cause. I thought it was a great idea, but I've been less than successful with money over the years, and I felt completely unqualified to co-host a financial podcast. Dave convinced me to do it anyway, and I figured that if I could be transparent and play the role of the "affable loser" that I could join Dave in good conscience. On 14 February 2021, we recorded our first episode. At the time that I'm writing this, we are getting ready to release our 117th episode. We have identified patterns in the stories of our guests and have created a framework for how middle-income earners might think about their money. This framework hangs on three imperatives, and the book is organized around them. The first imperative to financial success for the middle-income earner is to *be frugal*.

FRUGALITY

Being frugal means learning to live on less than you make. It is helpful if you can learn to be happy while being frugal. I know, I know, many think that the only way to be happy is to spend money like a spring breaker in Panama City in 1999. We are here to tell you that a fun life can be had on a budget. If you don't believe it, just keep reading.

One of the questions that we like to ask our guests on the show is whether they are wired as savers or spenders. Psychologically, we all seem to be wired one way or the other. For the saver, frugality comes naturally, but the spender needs to acquire the discipline necessary to constrain spending habits. To do this, a shift in mindset must occur. Money can purchase things, or money can purchase freedom. Think about it, are you a spender, or a saver? If you are married, is your spouse a spender or a saver? Knowing your money personality is critical, and it won't take much soul-searching to figure it out.

BUDGETING WITH A PURPOSE

When deciding how you will spend your money, you will need to identify what you value and what your goals are. Many of the guests on our show have expressed that purchasing freedom is a much better option for their money than buying "stuff." Making sure that you are saving and investing as much of your paycheck as possible will enable you to build wealth and work towards financial independence. Being financially independent means that you have enough wealth that you never have to work again. How soon would you like to become financially independent? The more money that you allocate towards your savings and investments the sooner you can achieve life without an alarm clock.

LIVE ON FAR LESS THAN YOU MAKE

Once you have learned to budget with a purpose, you better be careful. Building wealth is addictive. We have enjoyed hearing the testimonies over the last two years of teachers that have found ways to live on very little to maximize their income in the areas of saving and investing. In some cases, they are living extremely frugal lifestyles as a means to an end. They have decided to live on very little for a season to achieve financial independence. This concept is called "forced scarcity," and those that impose this on themselves, do so with a goal and a time frame in mind. I don't know if you can hear it, but your future self is cheering loud and proud for you to live on far less than you make.

WHO SAID A FRUGAL LIFESTYLE CAN'T BE FUN?

Do you have to drop $200 at a restaurant to have a good time on a date night? Must you have a $800 car payment to live a fulfilled life? Is a $10,000 family vacation to Disney necessary to make great memories? The answer to all these questions, and many more, is clearly "no." Sandwiches in the park make for a great date night, an affordable vehicle will take you where you need to go, and great memories can be made on a vacation almost anywhere. You can still enjoy life on a frugal budget if you choose to do so. Joy is a choice. We imagine that with a little more money we would be happy. This is an illusion. If you aren't happy spending $50,000 a year as a family, you won't be happy if you spend $100,000 per year. If you aren't convinced, give it a try. We dare you to attempt one weekend where you don't spend any money. Break out the bikes, wipe the dust off the old frisbee, or take a hike in a local state park. Financially, we love compound interest, but we have found the most satisfying form of compound interest comes from memories made with loved ones and friends. The best part? The memories only get sweeter with time.

LIVING A FRUGAL LIFESTYLE WITH A TWIST

We have interviewed many teachers that are financially successful, and all of them are living frugal lifestyles. We understand that as middle-income earners, resources are limited and there is little room for error. Middle-income earners must be wise and that means making some tough choices. Not all our guests have been frugal in the same way. Some drive very inexpensive cars, while at least one chooses to lease a new car every few years. Some never go out to eat, while others eat out on a consistent basis. A few of our guests don't go on vacations, while others travel frequently. The theme has been frugality with a twist. That twist is to discover what you value and give yourself permission to spend money where real value can be found. You can't have everything, but you can have some things. Dave Ramsey Personality George Kamel proudly proclaimed on the FIT podcast that he lives a "Bougie Frugal" lifestyle. According to George, being "Bougie Frugal" doesn't mean you can't visit New York City; it just means you might use public transportation from the airport to your hotel instead of Uber. The money saved can provide for a nice lunch the next afternoon, if that is what you value.

In the chapters under this first imperative, we will unpack the steps that need to be taken to live a frugal lifestyle, with a twist.

CHAPTER ONE
BUILDING YOUR BUDGET

"When you create a basic budget and stick to it,
it will suddenly seem like you have more money."
~Dave Ramsey

Many claim they have a budget, but do they really? Budgets must be written down and checked against actual spending on a regular basis. A budget cannot be an afterthought. Winning with money requires time, effort, sacrifice, and discipline. We have discovered that most people think that they are living on a budget, but very few are. If your budget isn't thought through, written down, and checked against actual spending on a regular basis, you aren't living on a budget. You have a rough idea, and you are winging it. Actively maintaining a budget is the main ingredient to a frugal lifestyle. If you fail to plan, you are planning to fail.

PERMISSION TO SPEND

We have found that when people don't care for the idea of budgeting, it is because they view budgets as restrictive joy stealers. The truth is a strict budget gives you permission to spend money. The first 20 years of my career, I spent money and then braced for impact. I thought I was living on a budget. I paid all my bills at the beginning of the month and then lived on whatever I had leftover. I took no thought for how much I was spending at any given moment. In my 20s, for example, I would take my wrestling team to off-season tournaments and pay for entry fees, food, gas, sometimes hotel rooms, and then go home and check my account balance to see if I had any money left. That is no way to live. There were many months that I had to live on credit cards, or do without, because I didn't have a real budget. That is a stressful life. Real joy comes from budgeting correctly so that when you do spend money, you can do it confidently.

THE ZERO-BASED BUDGET

The most popular method for budgeting in personal finance literature seems to be the Zero-Based Budget. There are other budgeting styles that you can research such as, "Pay Yourself First," the 50-30-20 Plan, or simply using a spreadsheet. Any of these will work, but Dave and I both use the Zero-Based Budget, and so that is the one that we are going to demonstrate.

Putting a Zero-Based Budget together is easy: you simply place how much your net income is at the top of your paper, and then subtract your savings, investments, bills, and expenses until you zero out the total that you began with. You will have given every penny an assignment. It is important to give every penny the RIGHT assignment. I used a Zero-Based Budget for years. I subtracted my bills from my monthly income, then I had what was left for living expenses. I allocated no money for savings or investing. I didn't think that I needed an emergency savings account. That was what my credit cards were for, right? I subscribed to the "don't leave home without it" motto. I am confident that not even my 22-year-old self would have actually made that argument, but I was living as though I believed that to be true. I would have argued that I had a budget, and I would have been wrong. What I had was an adult job, adult bills, adult expenses, and a child-like mentality. Real maturity is demonstrated best through responsibility. A good budget plan, where every penny is given the right assignment, accompanied by the will and discipline to execute that plan, is the best way to achieve financial independence.

The key to making the Zero-Based Budget work is to make sure that your spending reflects your values *and* your goals.

LINE-ITEMS IN YOUR BUDGET PLAN

It is important to come up with your personal list of line items. Some will be the same for everyone, while others will be unique to your budget. We probably all have a line-item for cell phones, but I have a line-item for books that many wouldn't have. When I first decided to get serious about budgeting, it was February 2020. I sat down and thought through all my monthly line-items and tried to determine how much to allocate for each. I didn't get my budget accurately locked in until May 2020. Be patient with yourself during this process. I would suggest going back three to six months in your checking account, and any other account that you use to make purchases and track your spending habits. This information will help you build a good budget. I went back six months in my checking account and discovered two things that I needed to do right away. The first thing that I did was cancel cable. I couldn't justify spending over $200 a month to watch TV. The world shut down for COVID during my second month of trying to execute a budget and that helped me to get my "eating out" line-item under control. I was spending way too much on eating out, and I knew that I was going to have to fix that bad financial habit. I was able to save over $500 a month by addressing these two issues.

THE CASH ENVELOPE SYSTEM

Sticking to a budget can be difficult when running a card for every purchase. Dave and Stephanie use the Cash Envelope System to avoid overspending in categories where the temptation to overspend or lose track of spending is common. Digital transactions rarely seem real. This is why humans tend to spend substantially more if they pay with plastic vs using cash. For this reason, we believe that the Cash Envelope System is a wonderful budgeting tool that can be used for line-items such as food, gas, sundries, spending money, etc. Dave and Stephanie are net-worth millionaires, and yet they still utilize the Envelope System. Ten years in, their envelopes are stuffed with more money now than when they first started out, and there are more envelopes in use than while they were in debt, but they have stuck with the system because it works. On the first of the month, Dave withdraws $2,000 from the bank to fill the envelopes. Next, Dave takes the cash and fills each designated envelope appropriately. The envelopes are budgeted to cover an entire month of spending. When an envelope for a category is out, it is out. This doesn't mean you can't repurpose your funds. Is it nearing the end of the month and the grocery envelope is empty? It is permissible to take money out of another envelope so the kids can eat. Even with the repurposing of envelope money, Dave and Stephanie always know they are spending $2,000 a month. Continually being able to see how much cash is left in each envelope helps to control spending. Here are their current monthly envelope categories and the total money allotted for each one every month:

1. **Groceries:** $800 (family of four, with two kids under 10)

2. **Eating Out:** $200 (dinners, fast food, pizza, and Sunday lunch after church)

3. **Gas:** $400 (Some don't enjoy going into the gas station to pay. Dave and Stephanie don't either, but they do it anyway.)

4. **Gifts:** $100 (often accumulates—birthday parties, baby showers, and the like.)

5. **Clothing:** $100 (this is for random basics, but does not include back to school shopping)

6. **Entertainment:** $200 (bowling, movies, and other family fun nights)

7. **Stephanie's Spending Money:** $100 (she can do whatever she wants with it)

8. **Dave's Spending Money:** $100 (he can do whatever he wants with it)

Dave and Stephanie stick to this system closely. Once they became debt free and achieved net-worth millionaire status, they took their foot off the gas pedal a bit, but as they were working towards those two goals, they were very strict on their budget allotments for each category. If attempting the Cash Envelope System, you will need to be patient with yourself. It might take a few months to get your envelopes set correctly. You might start with too much in one category or too little. Stick with it until you figure out the right balance.

My fiancée, Lori and I have decided to use the Cash Envelope System, too, but we are going to do it a little differently. We have decided to use cash for the following categories: groceries, eating out, gas, entertainment, and sundries (household items such as soap and paper towels). Instead of having five different envelopes for these items and filling all five envelopes up once per month, we will use one envelope and take out the amount that we are allowed to spend on these line-items weekly. Our budget for these will be $400 per week, but we are going to try to spend much less than that. We are both wired as spenders (I more than her) so we have decided to give ourselves an incentive to be frugal.

We like to travel, but our bucket-list is a little different from most. We are both Tar Heels born, and Tar Heels bred... we love the Tar Heel State! Our goal is to visit all 100 counties in North Carolina. We will take a weekend trip to a different county every time we save $1,000 out of our weekly envelopes. We are already plotting ways that we can cut our weekly spending in half so that we can take a weekend trip every five weeks.

Will this work for us? We don't know yet. We will get married one month from the published date of this book. Our plan is to try it, and then adjust if we discover that it doesn't work for us. The key to all of this is to be flexible as you work on what works best for your home.

SINKING FUNDS

A sinking fund is simply setting aside money for future expenses. It is a budgeting tool that we think should be employed by all middle-income earners. Rather than reacting to major expenses, plan. It is the FIT Position that you should allocate money to these accounts each month. As an example, if a new roof will be needed in ten years with a cost of approximately $20,000, start placing $166 per month in a sinking fund for this NOW. Sinking funds represent our best efforts to prepare for the future.

Almost everyone should consider the following five categories for sinking funds: (1) Christmas/December, (2) Vacations, (3) Home Maintenance or Mortgage Down Payment, (4) Future Automobile Purchase, (5) Summer Savings (especially for teachers that only get paid ten months per year).

I love the Christmas season. I love the "Christmas Season" sinking fund because I spend more money going out to eat, going to shows, and doing all things Christmas during the month of December. I spend more money at the grocery store (I'm a certified turkeyholic), and I buy decorations, gifts, and all things seasonal during this time of year. I have found that I spend an extra $1,500 from Thanksgiving to New Years. I put aside $150 each month for my "Christmas Season" sinking fund so that I can enjoy the season without guilt. Sinking funds can deliver peace of mind and joy to the middle-income earner.

Online banking institutions like Synchrony don't have brick and mortar branches; therefore, these banks tend to offer higher interest rates on savings accounts and make for a great option for parking your sinking funds. Before opening an account, make sure your online banking institution is FDIC insured.

PRACTICE MAKES PERFECT

Once you develop a budget plan it will take time to execute that plan well. You will make mistakes. It takes time to execute a budget, and you will probably never do it perfectly every month. During the first three to four months, you will be adjusting your plan and discovering what you really value. Be patient with yourself. Don't quit. Learn from each month and work on perfecting the craft of executing a perfect budget plan.

SEASONS OF YOUR LIFE

Life can get messy. We all know that staying out of debt, sticking to a budget, and being frugal is best; but sometimes life makes these endeavors difficult. What if you have a series of emergencies that cost more than the savings that you have in place? What if you go through a major change that leaves you with far less money to live on than you were accustomed to? What about rapid inflation?

I was cruising along for a time after becoming single again. I paid off all my debt and was in the process of building my emergency savings account when I started dating again. I always seem to be behind the learning curve, and I had a difficult time adjusting my budget to a new lifestyle of courting a woman. On the one hand, I spent more money than most would have deemed wise. On the other hand, we certainly found value in the experiences that we had together. At the time that I'm writing this, we are now engaged to be married and are working together to discipline our spending and to develop a financial plan that will put us in a position to build wealth in our married home.

As I am preparing to enter a season of my life where I will have a partner to build wealth with, I am reflecting on the season that I'm emerging from to learn from it what I can. I think that the key is to try and be as financially responsible as you can be in every season of life and fight the urge to throw caution to the wind. If you make a mistake, learn from it, and move on. Don't use the mistake as an occasion to quit. You will make mistakes, but don't get discouraged. The longer you allow yourself to make financial decisions out of discouragement, the deeper the hole that you will dig for yourself.

CHAPTER ONE ACTION STEPS

1. Pick a budget style. We recommend the Zero-Based Budget, but there are other budget systems that you might decide to use.

2. Determine what your household *net-income* is per month.

3. Determine what your bills and expenses are and create an exhaustive number of line items for your budget.

4. Start planning for future expenses and establish sinking funds.

5. Print off your credit and debit card statements from the last six months and get real with yourself to see where your money is going.

6. Go to the internet and search for "Budgeting Envelopes," and consider starting the cash envelope system. You can purchase pre-printed envelopes from places like Amazon and Etsy or create your own for free to fit the spending categories of your home.

CHAPTER TWO
EVALUATING YOUR BUDGET

*"If you don't get serious about your money,
you will never have serious money."*
~Grant Cardone

No matter what budgeting system you employ, we have developed the following seven categories to help you determine if your spending reflects your values. For a middle-income earner, all seven of the categories listed below should be considered when building your budget. We believe that you should determine how much of your income you should be spending in each category based on your goals and values. We can't offer a one-size-fits-all model here. It's called *personal* finance for a reason. What are your short-term goals? Long-term goals? What do you value? Your budget should reflect a thoughtful approach to your finances with these questions in mind.

Here is how it works: take all your line items and place them into one of the Seven FIT Budget Analysis Categories. All your spending will fit into one of the seven categories. Then add up each category. Finally, tally what percentage of your net-income is being allocated to each category. If you want to retire early, but you discover that less than 5% of your income is being invested, then you need to recalibrate your spending so that you can invest more. Do you place a premium on giving? Does your current budget reflect that value?

THE SEVEN CATEGORIES
TO EVALUATE YOUR BUDGET

Here are the seven categories. Again, we don't presume to be able to tell you how much you should be spending in each category. What we are including are the trends that we have discovered in the budgets of teachers that are winning with money to give you an idea of what you might need to do with your own budget.

1. **Giving:** a minimum of 10% has been mentioned by many of our guests. Dave and I both give 10% of our income to the church, and Dave and Stephanie even have a line-item in their budget called, "The Jesus Fund." They place 5% of their income in this fund and they use this money to be a blessing to others. Dave and I both believe strongly in the principle of giving, and so have many of our guests that are winning with money.

2. **Housing:** most of our guests spend between 20%-30% of their net income on housing. This includes their rent or mortgage (taxes & insurance included), and utilities. Some have spent far less than 20% and some have spent more than 30% of their net income on housing. Housing is one of the three major necessities that make up the bulk of spending for most (transportation and food being the other two). A great deal of consideration must be given in determining the percentage of your income that you can afford to commit to housing. You might be able to make a $2,000 mortgage payment, but you need to consider what this will do to your percentage breakdown and which category, or categories will be taken from to make that payment. You will then need to decide if you are comfortable with those sacrifices.

3. **Living Expenses:** this is the category most often cut by our guests. They look for ways to reduce the amount of income used in this category. Most of our guests spend less than 30% of their net-income on living expenses. Some are aggressive and are allocating less than 15% of their net income toward living expenses. Cutting back on eating out, cutting the cord on cable, and cutting off subscriptions to things like Netflix are just a

few examples where guests have reduced their living expenses.

4. **Debt Repayment:** this includes all debt outside of a mortgage. Some of the debts that are common are car notes, credit card debt, student loan debt, and personal loans. Some of our guests maintain car payments, some use credit cards at Christmas and then pay them back over the course of the next year, and many have or had student loan debt. Most of our guests that are winning with money have 0% of their total net-income allocated toward debt repayment outside of a mortgage. Before taking on debt, such as taking a loan out on a new car, you should look at the other categories to see if you can afford the extra debt. A large majority of our guests don't use credit cards and discourage others from using them. Not many that win with money have revolving debt. They might use a credit card, but they pay it off each month. We have had a few that use their credit card in this way to rack up reward points. This is a strategy that should only be employed by those who have proven to be disciplined over some length of time. If you must go into debt, have a plan to pay it off quickly. Don't let debt collect dust.

5. **Emergency Savings Account:** the rule on this is firm: you should have money for three to six months of bills and expenses in your ESA. After you achieve three to six months, you will probably want to allocate extra money each month or year to account for inflation. This isn't three to six months of salary but three to six months of your monthly bills and expenses.

6. **Sinking Funds:** these should always be considered. We have already mentioned sinking funds in the following areas: December/Christmas, Vacations, Automobiles, Home Maintenance, and Summer Savings for teachers. We also mentioned the example of a new roof in 10 years. What sinking funds do you need?

7. **Investing:** most of our guests are investing a minimum of 15% of their income in the stock market via retirement accounts or brokerage accounts. Many are also investing in real estate. The amount that you allocate towards investing will largely depend

on your retirement goals. Much more to come on investing under the fearless imperative.

BUILDING YOUR GAP NUMBER

Many middle-income earners are laboring under debt, and they are going deeper into debt each month because they are spending more money than they make. If this describes you, just know that you aren't alone. Millions are in the same boat. You will need to rewind your lifestyle to get your budget under control. Teachers are intelligent, creative, problem-solving people. To rewind a lifestyle that is not conducive to building wealth, you will have to utilize your talents to solve the unique problems that you face in putting your out-of-control lifestyle back in order.

To start this process, you should go back three to six months in your checking account (and any other accounts that you use to make purchases) and create a detailed account of where every penny is being spent. The amount of money taken in minus the amount of money that goes out in bills and expenses represents your gap number.

Your gap number is the amount of money that you have available to build wealth with. If your gap number is in the negatives, which probably means that a credit card is being used to get you through each month, this is a worse-case scenario and action must be taken immediately! If your gap number is in the negatives or zero, a lifestyle of living paycheck to paycheck is being executed, and this is dangerous. It only takes one or two tragic events to sink the financial well-being of a paycheck-to-paycheck actor. The goal is to have a gap number that is well above your total net-income so that you have plenty of money for giving, saving, and investing.

Increasing your gap number is always a good idea and can be achieved in three major ways:

1. Spending less money (Chapter Four)

2. Getting out of debt (Chapter Six)

3. Making more money (Chapter Seven)

FINANCIAL COACHING

Sometimes it is difficult to rewind a lifestyle that has produced spending habits that need to be corrected. It is rare for a financial advisor to work with individuals on basic budgeting exercises. Advisors generally want to work with clients who are ready to invest now because this is how they make money. This is why we believe in meeting with a good financial coach who can look at your financial situation and offer solid recommendations for how to get started in building your gap number. Sometimes a financial coach is only needed for a one-time meeting to get things rolling. In other cases, a coach might be needed for follow-up sessions to offer accountability and guidance.

Oftentimes financial coaches can come in and help couples get on the same page with their finances. The FIT Position is that most can benefit from the services of a good financial coach.

TRACKING YOUR NET WORTH

Websites such as Mint (https://mint.intuit.com/) or Empower (formally Personal Capital) can help you keep up with your budget, and can also assist in tracking your net-worth. Keeping up with your net worth is akin to keeping a scorecard and can be a motivating factor as you look to get out of debt and build wealth. Net worth is a simple equation: **Assets (home equity, investments, savings) minus liabilities (car notes, credit card debt, home loan) = Net Worth.**

Most of us graduate high school with zero net worth (we own nothing but owe nothing) and exit our 20s with a negative net worth (car debt, student loan debt). Many in America dream of being a "millionaire" but people are often confused about what that even means. A million-dollar net worth doesn't mean an individual or family MAKES a million dollars a year. It simply means that assets minus liabilities equal one-million dollars or more. Either way, our lives aren't defined by how many commas come after a series of numbers in our bank accounts, but keeping track of your net worth is a great way to measure growth and set goals for the future.

CHAPTER TWO ACTION STEPS

1. Go back through three to six months of activity in your checking account and any credit card accounts that you use and write down all expenses. The goal is to see how much money you spend and where you spend it.

2. Place all spending into the seven FIT Categories and find out what percentage of your money is currently being allocated to each category. Does the current breakdown reflect your goals and values well? Will your current breakdown result in building wealth?

3. Find out what your gap number is. You can't build wealth without a gap number. Look for ways to make it as large as possible.

4. Create a financial plan that will empower you to live according to the percentages that you are comfortable with. This might involve rewinding your current lifestyle. The perfect balance for you might take time to achieve. Your plan should be filled with short-term goals to help you reach the budget that you desire.

5. Create an account on Mint or Empower and start keeping up with your net worth.

6. If you are having trouble coming up with a plan that will work for you, having trouble executing a budget, or you and your spouse are struggling to agree on a budget, consider hiring a good financial coach. Hiring a good financial coach from the beginning can help you avoid the trial-and-error period that most go through on their own. As mentioned, Dave and I offer financial coaching. If you think that a financial coach could help you, visit us at www.financiallyindpendentteachers.com

CHAPTER THREE
BUDGET EXAMPLES

"The greatest wealth is to live content with little."
~Plato

"It's not the man who has too little,
but the man who craves more, that is poor."
~Seneca

"Beware of little expenses;
a little leak will sink a great ship."
~Benjamin Franklin

In this chapter we will be looking at a few budget examples so that you can see how the previous two chapters can be applied. Obviously, housing prices, cost of living, and incomes vary across the nation. We hope these examples can provide a framework for thinking about your own budget.

We are going to give you two eastern North Carolina examples. One of a single teacher that nets $3,000 per month. The second, a two-teacher household that nets $7,000 per month.

EXAMPLE #1

Budget Line-Items	Total Net-Income: $3,000	Evaluation Category
Tithe/Offering	-$300	Giving
Rent	-$850	Housing
Electric	-$150	Housing
Water, Sewage, & Trash Pickup	-$50	Housing
Phone	-$50	Living Expense
Internet	-$100	Living Expenses
Netflix	-$20	Living Expenses
Groceries	-$250	Living Expenses
Dining Out	-$100	Living Expenses
Sundries	-$100	Living Expenses
Gas	-$200	Living Expenses
Insurance	-$80	Living Expenses
Spending Money	-$100	Living Expenses
Car Payment	-$300	Debt Repayment
Emergency Savings Account (ESA)	-$300	Saving
Roth IRA	-$50	Investing
Total Left	**$0**	

BUDGET ANALYSIS

Giving	Housing	Living Expenses	Debt Repayment	ESA	Sinking Funds	Investing
$300	$1,050	$1,000	$300	$300	$0	$50
10%	36%	33%	10%	10%	0%	1%

As you can see, things are not easy for the teacher that is just starting out and single. If this is you, don't lose heart. Keep reading. This is only a season in your life, and there are things that you can do to make this season better.

The mechanics of this budget are correct, but is it a good budget? That isn't for me to decide. It depends on what this teacher values and what goals are being pursued.

I do have some questions for this teacher:

1. Have you considered a roommate that could cut your housing expenses in half?

2. How much longer do you have on that car note?

3. Would you consider taking all your "eating out" and "spending money" and making an extra "principle only" payment every month on your car until it is paid off?

4. With no summer sinking fund, how do you plan to get through the summer?

5. What sorts of insurance policies do you have? Do you have renter's insurance?

6. Are you looking for opportunities to make more money at your school, such as coaching, or administering the ACT?

7. Have you considered working a second job for a season so that you can get ahead?

8. Do you have a skill that you can parlay into a side-hustle?

As you continue to read through this book, you will see how coming up with a comprehensive plan to build wealth as a middle-income earner is very possible.

EXAMPLE #2

Budget Line-Items	Total Net Income: $7,000	Evaluation Category
Church Tithe/Offering	-$770	Giving
Mortgage (Taxes & Insurance Included)	-$1,100	Housing
Electric	-$200	Housing
Water, Sewage, & Trash Pickup	-$100	Housing
Internet	-$75	Living Expenses
Groceries	-$300	Living Expenses
Dining Out	-$100	Living Expenses
Sundries	-$150	Living Expenses
Gas	-$300	Living Expenses
Car Insurance	-$100	Living Expenses
Subscriptions (Netflix & Amazon Prime)	-$50	Living Expenses
Phones	-$115	Living Expenses
Spending Money	-$200	Living Expenses
Hair Appointment	-$140	Living Expenses
Car Payment	-$700	Debt Repayment
Emergency Savings Account (ESA)	-$500	ESA
Home Maintenance	-$300	Sinking Fund
Christmas	-$150	Sinking Fund
Vacation	-$250	Sinking Fund
Car	-$350	Sinking Fund
Vanguard Roth IRA	-$1,050	Investing
Total Left	**$0**	

BUDGET ANALYSIS

Giving	Housing	Living Expenses	Debt Repayment	ESA	Sinking Funds	Investing
$770	$1,400	$1,530	$700	$500	$1,050	$1,050
11%	20%	22%	10%	7%	15%	15%

As someone who has been single and trying to build wealth, I am fond of pointing out just how much easier it is to build wealth when you are married to another middle-income earner. If you look at this budget, you will notice that this couple's gap number is $2,600. To find this quickly you simply add up the ESA, Sinking Funds, and Investing categories; 37% of their total income is being used to save and invest. To be clear, the sinking funds are set up to be spent later, but just because they are earmarked to be spent, doesn't mean they have to be. Until the funds in those accounts are spent, they represent savings. This couple is investing 15% of their income. That is solid when compared to what many others are doing that win with money. This couple does have a large car payment. It represents 10% of their total income. Some would advise them to stop investing and throw every dime of that $1,050 on the car note. Dave and I don't believe that that is necessarily good advice. They are maxing out one Roth IRA, and almost maxing out another. If this couple is comfortable with 10% of their income going towards debt repayment, there is nothing inherently wrong with this budget plan. It is balanced.

A BALANCED BUDGET

I'm not talking about revenues being equal to or greater than total expenses (although that is the case here), I'm talking about the distribution of the funds across the categories. The amount of money that this couple is giving is solid, their housing costs and living expenses are reasonably low, although they have some debt... they aren't buried in debt by any stretch of the imagination, and they have a gap number that represents 37% of their income. They are close to paying all bills and expenses with one paycheck. Another stat I like to look at when evaluating budgets is the amount of money being spent on food. Again, the big-ticket items in any budget are housing, transportation, and food. This couple is spending less than 6% of their net-pay on food. That is outstanding.

LIVING ON ONE CHECK & SAVING/INVESTING THE REST

A great goal for any middle-income earning couple is to live off of one check and save &/or invest the other check. This isn't easy to do. It takes extreme frugality. Middle-income earning couples that are retiring early are finding a way to make this happen. Is the sacrifice worth it? That depends on your goals. What do you value most?

SUGGESTIONS FOR THIS COUPLE

The only thing that gives me pause with this budget is the large car payment. They have a sinking fund for their next automobile, so I'm guessing that once they pay off this car note, they might not have to go into debt for a car again. That is the hope. I would suggest that one of them take on a second job to pay that car off quickly. Especially if they have more than a year left on the loan. Freeing up $700 a month in their budget, or any middle-income earner's budget, is a big deal.

YOU BE THE FINANCIAL COACH

What should this couple do with the extra $700 that they will have once they pay off their car? There are certainly some wrong answers to this question, but there are also many right answers. If we gathered 20 people in a room to discuss this question, we would hear many good suggestions. The important thing for this couple to do is to recalibrate their budget with the extra $700 and give each penny of it the right assignment. In other words, they need to make sure that their percentage distribution reflects their goals and values with the extra $700 figured into new categories.

The worst thing that they can do is not be intentional with it. It's human nature to get sloppy with that kind of breathing room. Wealth-building opportunities are squandered when frivolous spending takes the place of fundamental budgeting practices.

CHAPTER THREE ACTION STEPS

1. Time to take the budget that you have built, and work on executing it.

2. Put your budget on a spreadsheet or paper and test it. Play around with the numbers and run projections for debt payoff. If you add an extra $100 to your car payment, how much sooner could you pay off your loan? If you cut $200 from groceries, where can you better apply the funds?

3. Continually reassess your bills and expenses. Once you get your budget where you feel comfortable, you must evaluate your numbers as new raises and life events transpire.

4. Read the rest of this book. There are many more things for you to consider. As you read further, we will introduce solutions to gap number and budgeting problems.

CHAPTER FOUR
SPEND LESS, SAVE MORE

"We make ourselves rich by making our wants few."
~Henry David Thoreau

The bottom line is that you must spend less than you make. Consumption rates must come down to maximize earnings. As mentioned in Chapter Two, your gap number is the money that you have left over each month, once spending is done. This is the amount of money that you have available to build wealth with. You should always be looking for ways to increase your gap number. Spending less per month is a good way to do this. There are several common areas where American middle-income earners spend too much money. Groceries, eating out, vehicles, vacations, Christmas, subscriptions, and online shopping are the most common culprits when it comes to over-consumption. In this chapter, we will explore some strategies for keeping these income gobbling areas under control.

GROCERIES

Dave has a family of four and he and his wife allocate $800 for groceries per month. It is common for a family of four to spend twice that per month on groceries. There are many reasons for this, but they all stem from not having a plan or not having the right plan when grocery shopping. Grocery shopping should be done once per week. If meals are planned there will be no need to make more trips to the grocery store during the week. The more trips that you make to the grocery store, the better the chances of you making unnecessary purchases. Here are some principles for putting together a good plan for the grocery store. These are only suggestions that have come from others who win with money. Maybe you can find some ideas in this list to adopt or perhaps these ideas will spark some of your own.

1. Keep meals simple and nutritionally dense. Nutritious meals are more filling.

2. Portion control. When too much money is spent on food, it is often because we are eating too much, which explains why so many of us are overweight. Even our kids are growing obese at younger and younger ages. The statistics on this are staggering.

3. You do not need meat every night. Meat is expensive and may be consumed too often. Beans and rice are cheap, easy to prepare, nutritionally dense, and filling. Eggs and potatoes make for another healthy, cheap meal. Other meals like pasta, or vegetarian plates that include three to four vegetables make for healthy, inexpensive meals.

4. Eliminate snacks and junk food that provide no nutritional value. Empty calories are a waste of money. While you are at it, get rid of the sodas and sugary drinks that provide no nutritional value and suck up your income. Water is best for you and is the cheapest thing to drink. Bored with water? Add flavoring to your water and consider coffee or tea.

5. Meal Plan! Use coupons and store sales to build your meal plans for the week. If you are going to eat meat, try to get it on sale. Plan your meals for the entire week and cook on Sundays to avoid needing to be bailed out by fast food on a weeknight.

6. Utilize leftovers for lunch. Do not waste food. You can make dinner with leftovers for lunch in mind.

7. Breakfast gets expensive when buying junk food that doesn't make for a good breakfast anyway. A large bag of potatoes and 24 eggs will feed a family of four for at least a week and costs very little.

8. Popcorn is a good, cheap snack.

9. Do not fall into the trap of giving your children choices. Put good food in front of them. They can eat or starve. They will eventually eat. We are raising picky, entitled kids, and spending a fortune catering to their delicate junk food desiring palates. Kids do not know what is best for them. They should not be given choices.

10. Eat meals together as a family. This is a great opportunity to spend time with your children. You can discuss all sorts of things including the day's events and what's on everyone's mind. It will also enable your family to talk about personal finances, the cost of food, and the importance of budgeting.

Conversations about diet can be difficult between couples. Back in 2021 I was dangerously overweight. My doctor told me that if I didn't make some drastic changes, I was going to be dramatically shortening my life. I'm a former wrestler (if you know then you know) so I went into weight cutting mode in 2022. Through trial and error, I found a system that worked for me and a meal schedule that I could execute, and I lost approximately 85 lbs. during the 2022 calendar year. During that time, I didn't view food as something to be enjoyed. It was simply fuel that I had to have to keep going. I was not only losing weight but saving a great deal of money at the grocery store. I was spending as little as $20 per week and eating nutritionally dense meals. I went to the extreme, and I would love to continue that throughout my life. On the other hand, I would like to not remain single for the rest of my life, so some compromise will be in order. Determining a food budget and meal plan with your significant other is "low key" tricky. It will probably take some time to iron out the balance between the idea that food is for enjoyment, and the idea that food is for fuel.

EATING OUT

As a society, we have become very liberal in the frequency by which we patronize restaurants. Eating out is expensive and when done regularly, is a major roadblock to building wealth. When in the wealth-building phases of life, eating out should not be the norm. When getting out of debt, eating out should rarely happen. Cutting off restaurants could be the catalyst for a more intense and faster path to becoming debt free. The FIT Position is to have a tight food budget and to eat most meals at home. Looking back at Chapter One, we recommended an "Eating Out" envelope to help budget eating out habits. Dave and his wife have achieved a level of financial success and their monthly eating out envelope is $200 per month. When they started, it was only $100. Once out of debt, it is permissible to add more if this is something you really value.

When combining the amount of money spent on groceries and eating out, the average family spends at least twice the amount that they should on food. In addition to eating meals at restaurants, you must consider fast food spending, gas station snacks and drinks, Starbucks coffee, etc. Many families could fully fund a Roth IRA on the money they spend dining out. If you want to increase your gap number, remember what our parents would always say when we asked for McDonalds on the road: "No. We have food at home."

VEHICLES

The loan amounts being taken out for cars are truly out of control in America. People are routinely spending $500 - $900 a month, or more, on vehicle payments. This is madness. If you invested that amount of money, it would be worth hundreds of thousands of dollars in the future. Instead of earning interest, interest is being paid on a vehicle that started depreciating the moment it was driven off the lot. It is the FIT Position to avoid car payments, if possible. Money should be placed in a sinking fund monthly for the next car purchase, and whatever amount has been accumulated in that fund is the budget for the next car. Strive to pay cash for vehicles. If you must finance one, set a goal for a 20% down payment and pay it off as fast as you can. Once your vehicle is paid off, utilize the strategy of a sinking fund, and start saving for your future "next" vehicle. If you have buried yourself in car payments, explore the possibility of selling and downsizing.

A middle-income earner cannot build wealth when paying a ridiculous amount of money on a car note every month. Remember, you are not what you drive. A financial superpower is not caring what anyone else thinks of your social status.

Here are a few checks to see if the amount you are spending on vehicles is out of balance:

1. You spend more on monthly car payments each month than you save/invest.

2. The purchase price of your vehicle is around the same amount as your annual gross income per year.

VACATIONS

Everyone wants to go to Disney. If not Disney, many would spend thousands of dollars going to some other destination because they imagine the more money they spend, the more fun they will have and the better memories that they will make. You can make great memories and have a wonderful time doing all sorts of things that will not cost you anywhere near the amount of money that a trip to Orlando will cost you. It is possible to make memories and have fun while spending very little.

No matter where you plan to go for vacation, have a sinking fund that you contribute to each month to pay for it. Should you decide that a pilgrimage to see the famous mouse is an experience that cannot be missed, it might take a long time to save for that. Using a credit card should not be an option. If you do not have the cash to cover the cost of a trip, do not go. It is that simple. Vacations should be enjoyable. They are less enjoyable when they eat up your savings and increase your debt levels which in turn, create buyer's remorse. Using the sinking fund strategy is a great way to save for a future trip. Want to go on a trip that will cost $2,400 a year from now? Simply, save $200 per month and pay cash. Bring your trip home with you in the form of pictures and memories, not high interest payments and bills in the mailbox.

CHRISTMAS

I just checked my calendar, and sure enough Christmas will happen on December 25th again this year. Credit cards are utilized during the Christmas season more than any other time during the year. It is as if people are taken by surprise and must react by paying interest on toys that will be broken before the bill is paid in full. Set up a sinking fund for Christmas and whatever you have in that fund is what your Christmas budget is.

When buying for your kids, here is a great guiding principle:

1. Buy something to wear
2. Buy something to read
3. Buy something they want
4. Buy something they need
5. Buy something to eat

Do not borrow from your future self to pay for Christmas every year. Plan for it, set a budget for it, and stick to the plan. Overspending at Christmas time is a gap number killer!

SUBSCRIPTIONS

These can add up. The amount paid per subscription is often cheap enough to go mostly unnoticed until adding them up and seeing that they account for more than $200 a month. Netflix, Hulu, Amazon Prime, magazines, monthly book subscriptions, dollar shave club, the jelly of the month club, etc. can really add up and kill your gap number. Sometimes married couples will discover that they are both paying for a Netflix subscription. Some are surprised to find out that $200 - $300 a month is going out the window for subscriptions that they do not value and barely use. Cancel these subscriptions.

ONLINE SHOPPING

The "Add to Cart" option is a gap number killer. It has become so easy to buy things which we have no need. There was a time when a trip to a mall or shopping center was required to throw our money away. Now we can throw our money away from the comfort of our own living room. Amazon even makes recommendations of things never thought of but must be purchased once seen.

Only spend what is in the budget. In addition, we recommend the 24-hour rule. Never buy anything until it has been in your online cart for at least 24 hours. This rule will help in avoiding some of the ridiculous purchases that might be made without thinking.

CREDIT CARDS

The FIT Position is that you should not carry revolving debt. Never put something on a credit card that can't be paid off IMMEDIATELY.

There might come a time in your financial journey where you utilize credit cards for travel rewards points, but this is a next-level strategy that should only be utilized by people who are GREAT with money, are not in debt of any kind, and have already built a substantial amount of wealth. These people are using the credit card as a tool, not a way to increase their lifestyle without being able to afford it. The number of people that can check off all those boxes is low. With that in mind the FIT Position is to leave the credit cards in your wallet and pay cash or do without. Credit card debt will destroy your gap number.

CHAPTER FOUR ACTION STEPS

1. Create meal plans each week that will enable you to stick to your grocery budget.

2. Be aware of how much money you are spending eating out.

3. Pay cash for vehicles. Pay off the car notes that you currently have, and then start a sinking fund for future automobile purchases. You might even be able to sell current vehicles to get out of debt faster.

4. Set up a sinking fund for future vacations so that you can pay cash for them. Be reasonable with where you go. Until you are debt free, there will be no vacations.

5. Set up a sinking fund for Christmas so that you can pay cash for Christmas gifts and expenses. Stick to the budget.

6. Go through all your subscriptions and cancel those that add little to no value to your life. That will be most of them.

7. Stop making silly purchases whether online or not. If you are in debt, you have no money for extra stuff, and you cannot build wealth buying things which you can do without. If you are debt free, set a reasonable limit for spending money and stick to the budget.

8. Pay off your credit cards and never carry revolving debt

CHAPTER FIVE
FLIPPING LIFESTYLE CREEP

"Plain and simple, lifestyle creep is when your income goes up and your spending creeps right up to meet it. You don't even notice the shift. It just happens."
~Rachel Cruze

Lifestyle creep happens slowly over time. We often do not recognize it at first. When your gap number increases, it is natural to become more liberal with your spending. Beware of falling into the trap of receiving a raise and rather than recalibrating your budget to account for the extra income, you just end up spending it. If you stop checking your spending against your budget, what was once a perfectly executed plan is now off track. It might only be off by a little at first but can become a huge mess whereby opportunities to build wealth have been replaced with frivolous spending. Is there a worse feeling than spending $100+ and you can't even remember what you spent it on?

HEALTHY ROUTINES

There are three routines that you can develop that will assist you as you attempt to maintain discipline in your budgeting habits. They work down from annual, to monthly, to daily. If you establish these routines, you will find them to be instrumental in your fight against lifestyle creep.

1. **Plan Your Budget for The Year:** Go through each month and look at what expenses will be unique to each month and plan

accordingly. Keep notes on your calendar of things that you missed that you can use to tighten up your calendar next year. An annual budget will give you a vision for your saving and investing goals and provide a renewed sense of the value that a budget brings to your life. It will also give you an opportunity to adjust your monthly budget categories to accommodate any raises that you receive. For teachers, this might be done in July or August of every year. For other middle-income earners, this might be best accomplished in December. If you are married, this should be done with your spouse. Oftentimes one person in a marriage takes charge of the finances while the other is largely uninvolved. There is nothing inherently wrong with this; however, the annual budget plan should be done together.

2. **Monthly Budget Review:** Carve out an hour of your time at the end of each month to review your budget for the upcoming month and to check on how you did the previous month. In addition, review the annual budget. The habit of reviewing the annual budget each month will help to keep you on track so that you can accomplish your annual goals. If you are married, this monthly budget meeting should be done together.

3. **Daily Review:** Take 15 minutes every day to check your spending against your budget. This will probably not take 15 minutes of your time, and it is a daily habit that will pay huge dividends. By looking at spending and the budget plan daily, you will always have your guard up against undisciplined habits that tend to creep in under the radar. If you are married, this does not have to be done together. The person that is primarily responsible for the family budget can do this on their own.

WHAT TO DO WITH RAISES OR OTHER FINANCIAL WINDFALLS?

If you are in debt (other than your mortgage), there is only one thing to do with extra money and that is to throw most of it on your debt. If you are debt free without a full emergency savings account, toss the extra money into that bucket UNTIL you reach your three-to-six-month ESA number.

The FIT Position involves spending money where you find value and developing the habits of saving, investing, and giving. For teachers, raises are not often that significant. Perhaps you are receiving a bump in pay that is going to result in $120 extra in your monthly net pay. Be intentional, even with small amounts of money. That $120 monthly raise gives you a new net-income level and so your percentages will need to be recalibrated. You can divide the extra money over several categories or place it all into one. Just make sure that after you have applied the extra money your percentage breakdown still reflects your goals and values.

Being intentional with extra money from a raise is essential. No matter how small the raise is, have a plan for it. Remember, the goal is to make sure that every penny serves a purpose and has the right assignment. Now that Dave and his wife are debt free, he uses raises to increase his giving, investing, and lifestyle by a little each.

CATCH LIFESTYLE CREEP AND FLIP THE DIRECTION

Raises often lead to unnecessary larger homes and nicer vehicles. One of the keys to the success that Dave and Stephanie have achieved was putting a pause on lifestyle creep. Like many Americans, Dave and Stephanie "moved up" in home once they had their two children. Having children led to the couple purchasing a 5-bedroom, 3.5 bath 3,600 square foot home in suburbia, filled with teachers and other middle-income earners. Even worse, after living in their much larger home for a few years, they were ready to upgrade again and made an offer on a 4,000 square foot house that was listed for $500,000. Fortunately, their offer of 475k was rejected. After some soul searching, they still decided to move. This time, they did a 180 and went down in lifestyle. The 3,600 square foot home was put on the market and the couple downsized to a 2BR/2BA-900 square foot townhouse. After running the numbers, Dave realized they could use the equity from their large home, pay cash for the 40-year-old townhouse and complete $15,000 worth of upgrades to bring the house into the 21st century. Gone was the two-car garage (down to one), the movie room, the guest bedrooms, and separate bedrooms for the children. These sacrifices were worth it because they were also able to dump their $1,500 per month mortgage payment and save an additional $250 per month in reduced utility costs. This was their fork in the road moment ...they were so close to being in a $500,000+ gated community, but instead they chose a C+ townhome neighborhood that was full of rental properties, many of which were in desperate need of attention. They no longer live in that townhouse, but it did produce $20,000 net income for them last year as a short-term rental property!

Instead of letting lifestyle creep steal your wealth-building opportunities, flip the script, and take your lifestyle the other way! The less you spend, the more that you can give, save, and invest! The Joneses are broke, don't try to keep up with them.

CHAPTER FIVE ACTION STEPS

1. Keep an annual budget on a calendar and if you are married, do the annual budget together.

2. At the end of each month review the month just completed, preview the month ahead, and review the annual budget to check progress. If you are married, do this together.

3. Carve out 15 minutes each day to check spending against the budget to ensure discipline. If you are married this can be done by the one that is primarily responsible for the family finances.

4. Develop a strategy for money gained through raises.

5. Look at your future salary schedule and try to prepare for the likely raises that will be coming.

6. Check yourself. Are you inflating your lifestyle to keep up with the Joneses?

CHAPTER SIX
BEATING DEBT

"The borrower is slave to the lender."
~**Proverbs 22:7**

Debt is the dirtiest four-letter word in the dictionary. The fact is that teachers can build wealth, but on a fixed income there is no room for error. Debt can be a major error. Going into debt is normal in America, and so is being broke. Don't be normal.

Living a debt-free lifestyle is a habit. Going into debt for things is also a habit. We need to avoid the temptation of going into debt. For example, many well-intentioned and otherwise frugal people will look at their budget and conclude that they can afford a big car payment. Perhaps they can, but not without paying a price. The money being spent on debt is money that you cannot invest or save. Your money will either purchase things, or it will purchase freedom. The FIT Position is to live a debt-free lifestyle so that you can spend your money purchasing financial independence. Our grandparents had a novel idea about spending... if you don't have the money on hand to pay for it, you can't buy it! Delayed gratification makes purchases that much more special. You might even find that you don't want "it" anymore after you decide to start saving for an extended period of time.

SPENDERS V. SAVERS

As mentioned in Chapter One, most people are wired as either spenders or savers. Those of us wired as spenders have a difficult time sticking to a budget and staying out of debt. Knowing which one of these you best identify with will not take much soul-searching. It will be obvious to you. If you are a spender, or if your spouse is a spender, it is important to impose rules on your spending habits to stay debt free. These same rules are great for savers as well, but savers probably abide by these rules naturally.

RESPONSIBLE SPENDING

The following is a collection of advice that has been given by multiple guests on our podcast:

If it is not in the budget, you cannot have it. Tapping into your savings account is not an option. That is for emergencies only. Emergencies are for extreme events. If your electronic awning breaks, that does not constitute an emergency. Take it down and buy an umbrella.

Beware of credit cards. Paying cash is better than going into debt. Again, if it isn't in the budget, you can't have it. Credit cards will never be used unless a true emergency occurs and you do not have enough in savings to cover the cost. Credit cards are dangerous, and they usually come with high interest rates. The decision to use one in an emergency should cause grief and should be a very last resort.

Plan for major purchases and utilize sinking funds for these. We covered this in Chapter One, but it is worth repeating; contribute monthly to sinking funds for things that you know that you will need money for in the future.

Try to never purchase anything on a whim. Wait 24 hours before making any purchases, even if you have enough budgeted spending money to cover the purchase.

If you are married, never make a major purchase without talking it over with your spouse. If your spouse does not think that the purchase is a good idea, shelve it. A couple should agree on all major purchases. A couple should also agree on what constitutes a large purchase. If one spouse thinks $250 is a large purchase but the other thinks a large purchase is $1,000, this could lead to bigger issues.

WHAT IF I AM ALREADY IN DEBT?

If you are reading this and your current debt situation is not good, do not lose heart. There are many in your predicament and many more that have made their way out of the dark night of debt and into the light. While there might be other strategies employed for getting out of debt, the FIT Position is to utilize one of two. First, there is the *Dave Ramsey Debt Snowball Approach*. This approach helps you to build momentum and gives you the psychological edge needed to keep moving forward. Second, there is the *Debt Avalanche Approach*. This approach is for those that get hung up on the numbers and don't need to see immediate progress to achieve a psychological edge.

DAVE RAMSEY DEBT SNOWBALL APPROACH

You list all your debts, smallest to largest (excluding your home). You make the minimum payments on all of them, but you take all your extra money (your gap number) and place it on the smallest debt that you have until you pay that debt off. Once it is paid off, your gap number grows and so you can place even more money on the next debt on the list. You very quickly achieve a snowball effect. This is a great strategy and has worked for many. Psychologically, this enables you to see quick wins and keep the momentum going to pay off the next debt.

DEBT AVALANCHE APPROACH

Another strategy is to do the same thing but list your debt in order of the highest interest rate to the lowest. The argument is that this makes the most sense mathematically. The trouble is that it might take you longer to get that first debt paid off. If that doesn't discourage you, the Debt Avalanche might be the best method for you.

DEBT CONSOLIDATION

There are other strategies that involve debt consolidation, but we do not recommend any of these. The FIT Position is to execute one of the two strategies mentioned and get to work. While I was in my 20s, I got myself into credit card debt. The debt was spread out over four different high interest credit cards. I decided to take out a personal loan at a lower interest rate and pay off the credit cards, consolidating my debt into one lower monthly payment. I felt good about the strategy, but what I failed to do was correct the behavior that put me in that debt position to begin with. I still had a wrestling team to fund and a terrible habit of eating out too often and I wound up running all those credit cards back up again. To get out of debt, I ended up taking a job at a gas station and placing all the extra money on my debt. I dreaded every shift that I worked at that gas station. It was painful to take all that extra money and give it to those lenders. I came to discover that stupidity should be painful. I would love to report that the pain of that experience prevented me from doing more stupid things in the future, but unfortunately, I have a high tolerance for pain.

NEGOTIATE WITH YOUR CREDIT CARD COMPANY

Remember the "phone a friend" option on the TV show *Who Wants to Be a Millionaire*? Believe it or not, credit card companies will often work with you on your debts, especially if you are really struggling financially. Give them a call. They might take the stance that getting something in the form of a payment is better than nothing at all. A member of the FIT Family once had $15,000 of credit card debt and made the dreaded phone call to a representative of their favorite plastic safety net. After a short conversation during the first phone call, the credit card company obliged and decided to freeze their 18% interest rate for six months. After six successful months of paying on the debt (with no interest), they made another call. This time, the company said they would cut the debt in half from $12,000 to $6,000, IF they made monthly $1,000 payments until the debt was completely paid off. While not a guarantee, phoning a friend never hurts anyone.

CHANGING YOUR LIFESTYLE TO GET OUT OF DEBT

If you are currently in debt, there is plenty of hope for you. There are some things that you need to do: first, while getting out of debt, most of your extra money should go toward your debt. There are no luxuries to be enjoyed while you are in debt as a teacher or middle-income earner. No vacations. No eating out. No going to the movies. Your entire gap number and all extra money earned will be spent on getting out of debt. The faster you get out of debt, the earlier you can start to enjoy life again. Remember, this is only for a season, and this season of your life will end and give way to a better, debt free season. The more aggressive you are, the faster freedom comes.

Next, spend as little as possible on gas, food, and sundries. Suffer for a little while and live the rest of your life debt free. Eat only the basics and eat at home. Skip the name brand sundry items. Stay home and only use gas to get to work and back. Cancel cable, internet, house phones... anything that is a luxury that can be cut, cut it. Again, these sacrifices are temporary and lead to freedom.

You might also consider selling off items that you do not need. Have a garage sale, utilize Facebook Marketplace or some other online marketplace. If you owe too much on a car, try to sell it and secure a smaller debt or no debt on a cheaper car. Get creative.

Finding ways to make more money and creating multiple streams of income is a well-advised strategy for getting out of debt. Getting out of debt is painful. No need to stretch this season of your life out any longer than you must. Working a second job might be miserable, but it will help you pay off your debt faster. In Chapter Seven we list possibilities for creating multiple streams of income. Execute as many of these strategies as possible. Look for ways to make more money and place all extra money made on your debt.

The state of North Carolina has a website whereby you can look to see if anyone owes you any money. If you live in another state, see if there is a service like this provided to you. Many will find that they have money owed to them that they just need to claim. In North Carolina the website is: https://www.nccash.com/. Put any funds that you can claim on your debt. In addition, tax returns, stipends, or any other income garnered throughout the course of the year should be placed on your debt.

It is easy to let up when your debt levels start coming down. Our advice is that once you gain momentum, do not take your foot off the pedal. Letting your guard down is a mistake. Stay on the attack.

STAYING OUT OF DEBT

You must budget, budget, budget! Every penny of your income needs the right assignment and be sure to maintain a healthy emergency savings account and utilize those sinking funds. Sinking funds are a product of thinking ahead. Every year you should think through the calendar. Think ahead and reduce the number of times that you are blindsided by bills or expenses that you were not prepared for. In addition, live a minimalist lifestyle. There are many more teachers that are net-worth millionaires than you might think. They live in 1600-2000 square foot homes, drive low-key vehicles, wear modest clothes, eat most of their meals at home, and take modest vacations. They happily move through life because they are financially secure.

BE A TEAM

If you are married, you and your spouse should be partners on the same mission. You win with money together. Sometimes couples have a difficult time working out a budget and financial goals together. We cannot stress enough the value that a financial coach can bring to your team. A financial coach can help you see things that you missed in your budget, offer accountability, help you and your spouse to get on the same page, and offer suggestions for building wealth that you might not have thought of otherwise.

GET YOUR DEBT SITUATION UNDER CONTROL

Teachers can build wealth. There are different paths to financial independence for teachers, but they all have this in common: they include a lifestyle where debt is under control. Your income will be used to build wealth for someone. The only question is will you build wealth for yourself or someone else? Most of our guests live a debt-free lifestyle. Those that do go into debt are very careful not to allocate too much of their income toward debt repayment.

CHAPTER SIX ACTION STEPS

1. Impose rules for spending that will help you to stay out of debt.

2. If you are currently in debt, execute either the Debt Snowball or the Debt Avalanche.

3. Execute a budget well for a long period of time and become intimately aware of your financial situation and what you can and can't handle financially.

4. Call your credit card company and ask to freeze your interest or strike up a deal to pay your debt off faster.

5. Any extra money that comes in (tax money, bonus, stipends), throw most of it on your debt.

6. Don't give up!

IMPERATIVE #2
BE FEARLESS

"Everything you want is on the other side of fear."
~Jack Canfield

On the podcast, we relate many things to sports. Brandon and I both participated in collegiate athletics and we've each coached a handful of different sports at the high school level. Having a balanced offensive and defensive game plan is desirable in most sports, and it is also desirable in the world of personal finances. Imperative #1 focused on defensive money strategies to guard against overspending and debt to help build a healthy gap number. A healthy gap number is needed to go on the offensive. Imperative #2 will focus on the offensive side of money. Being Fearless is what is needed to parlay your healthy gap number into a wealth building machine. We talked about why Imperative #1 is so difficult for those wired as spenders. Well, Imperative #2 is difficult for those wired as savers. Savers often have no trouble with frugality, but when it comes to investing and putting their savings at risk, they will have to muster all of their courage, and with a sweat beaded forehead, just do it. The spender has the advantage here as they will often just redirect their spending habits and purchase investments instead of more "stuff." If they are investing in the stock market, for example, they are simply adding shares to their investment firm's cart rather than Amazon's. With a big grin on their face, they let it ride. I suppose that it is only fair that no matter how you are psychologically wired, you will have challenges to overcome on your journey to financial independence. Spenders must learn to be frugal. Savers must learn to be fearless.

TO BUILD WEALTH YOU WILL
LIKELY NEED TO DO TWO THINGS

1. **Create multiple streams of income.** Many of the teachers interviewed on the FIT podcast have created multiple streams of income to win with money. To do this, you might have to do some things that you have never done before, such as taking on more responsibility at work, starting a business, or working a second job. This will require you to make some dramatic changes in your lifestyle and run the risk of failure. Change is scary, and the potential to fail is even scarier. You will need to be fearless if you want to build wealth.

2. **You will need to invest.** You can invest in the stock market, the real estate market, or both, but in any case, you will need to invest to maximize your gap number and build wealth. This is a scary proposition because you run the risk of losing your money. All markets are volatile, and you will take losses on your way to financial independence. Investors must be fearless.

A FEW POINTS THAT HELP YOU
BECOME MORE FEARLESS

1. Starting your own business or taking on a second job can be scary and fear is one of the most powerful human emotions. On the other hand, if you always do what you have always done, you will always be what you have always been. With that in mind, what do you have to lose?

2. If you avoid the risk of investing and store up your money in cash or a savings account, you are guaranteed to lose your money. The interest rate that your money will earn in a savings account will be far less than the rate of inflation. Your money will lose spending power over time sitting in a savings account. That is a guarantee.

3. Although the stock market and real-estate markets can be volatile in the short term, in the long term they've always increased in value. Even adjusted for inflation, the S&P 500 rendered a 7.42% return from 1950-2023, which includes many global crises. The average historical rate of return given by the total stock market is just north of 10% and that includes world wars, pandemics, crashes, and downturns. Investing in the stock market or real estate is not a get-rich-quick scheme. It takes time and pressure to build wealth by investing. A savings account has its place, but it is very difficult to build wealth and financial independence on a product that doesn't keep up with inflation. To get an 8%-12% rate of return, you must be fearless!

Look at the two charts to see the difference between decades worth of savings vs. decades worth of being fearless and investing. The chart assumes a high yield savings account with Synchrony, where you can currently get a 4%+ interest rate. *Past performance results are not indicative of future results.*

Initial Investment	Years	Rate of Return	Growth	Total
$1,000	10	4% (Savings)	$480	$1,480
$1,000	10	10% (Investing)	$1,593	$2,593

Initial Investment	Years	Rate of Return	Growth	Total
$10,000	40	4% (Savings)	$38,010	$48,010
$10,000	40	10% (Investing)	$442,592	$452,592

We often hear teachers quip that rates of return this high don't exist. If you don't believe us, just Google "S&P 500 rate of return since 1950" and see the results for yourself.

4. The tax shelters and investment products available to us as middle-income earners make it seem foolish not to invest. More to come on this.

The path that seems scary has been taken by many before you and those that stayed the course became financially independent. Perhaps on the strength of their testimonies you can overcome your fears and follow the FIT Position.

"Be fearful when others are greedy,
and be greedy when others are fearful"
~Warren Buffet

No matter how you do it, you can't build wealth while sitting on the sidelines. You must be fearless.

CHAPTER SEVEN
CREATE MULTIPLE
STREAMS OF INCOME

"Business opportunities are like buses;
there's always another one coming."
~Nick Loper

Teachers are in a unique position to make extra money. We typically work 190-200 days per year, and for many, contract hours end early in the afternoon. Once you have increased your gap number by reducing spending and getting out of debt, you should turn your attention to increasing your gap number by making more money. Of course, these things can be accomplished simultaneously. It is the FIT Position to constantly look for multiple streams of income as a teacher. We have enjoyed hearing all of the different and creative ways that teachers have been able to make extra money with the extra time that they have as educators.

MAX OUT YOUR EARNING POTENTIAL
AT YOUR CURRENT JOB

Before stepping outside of the schoolhouse, it is important to understand the income maximization opportunities that are available to us through our careers as educators. Most states offer pay incentives for teachers who have advanced degrees beyond their bachelor's degree. Many states provide a 10%-12% salary increase for a master's degree. Having additional education hours beyond a master's degree (+15 hours, +30 hours, Ph.D.) will give a significant pay increase in many districts. In addition, 32 states give an additional pay bump for teachers who become National Board Certified. In North Carolina, NBPTS certification provides a 12% salary increase. For example, a teacher in North Carolina that is Nationally Board Certified (which can be earned after three years of experience) will make over $125,000 more over the course of their career than a teacher without the certification. It is not easy, but most teachers say it is worth the effort. Several guests on our podcast have become net-worth millionaire educators by maxing out their earning potential with a master's degree and becoming nationally board certified. Look at what you can do to max out your earning potential in the state and school district that you are in. Not only will maxing out your earnings via these additional credentials help in the here and now, but it will also significantly impact your monthly pension in retirement as well.

EARNING EXTRA MONEY IN THE SCHOOL HOUSE

Depending on the state that you teach in, you might be able to earn extra money covering classes, giving up your planning period, teaching drivers ed, acting as a peer mentor, leading a club, coaching a sport, administering standardized tests, driving a bus, running prom, etc. Many teachers that we have spoken with take these opportunities to earn extra money to build wealth. These are not only great ways to increase income but are also great ways to build rapport with students and community stakeholders.

LOCAL SUPPLEMENTS

Many school districts offer local supplements to recruit and retain teachers. In both of our cases, the counties we work in offer a 12% local supplement. Even though the state pay scale may suggest we make $52,000 per year, the local supplement offers an additional $6,240 pay increase. Rather than blowing this money, be intentional with it. Use the extra income to aggressively get out of debt, build your ESA, invest, or even treat yourself to something nice. Raising your income by participating in many of the above activities will also increase your monthly pension in retirement.

TEACHING OUT OF THE COUNTRY

We have interviewed multiple teachers that have moved out of the country to take advantage of the wealth building benefits associated with teaching in foreign schools. Many have taught in low-cost living areas while paying little to no taxes and making more money. Some of these assignments come with free housing. Even if this strategy is only utilized for a few years, it can give a teacher just the boost that they need in their financial journey.

A PART TIME JOB—WORKING FOR THE MAN

With late afternoons, holidays, and summers off, there are plenty of extra hours by which a teacher might pick up a second job to earn extra money. While a part-time job can be worked at any age, the time to rack up the hours is when you are younger and have more energy and potentially less responsibility. Working a part-time job and banking the money made is a great way to build wealth. Working a part-time job isn't easy, and it might not be a sustainable endeavor over a long period of time. Perhaps you can take on a part-time job with a specific purpose in mind? Brandon once took on a part-time job with the goal of paying off credit card debt. Once he paid off the debt, he resigned. No one in the world could have been happier than Brandon when he clocked out of that job for the last time.

Working for a large box store such as Wal-Mart or Target might also provide an additional passive income source such as a company 401(k) match and discounted shopping.

A SIDE HUSTLE—WORKING FOR YOURSELF

Teachers are very talented people that generally have a skill set that can be marketed and guided into a lucrative business. Many teachers have even parlayed their side hustle into a permanent move away from teaching, going into business for themselves full-time. In our interviews on the FIT Podcast, we have heard the stories of teachers that have started all sorts of businesses. One teacher runs his own pressure washing business; another owns his own bouncy house business; a few tutor on the side; one runs wrestling tournaments in the spring and summer; another owns his own lawn care business. All these businesses are examples of a side hustle, and supplement the income of these teachers, creating a larger gap number for themselves. What kind of a business could you start that might be a game-changer for you financially?

HOUSE HACKING

This is a great way to make extra money. Have an extra bedroom in your house? Maybe you have an ADU (accessory dwelling unit) above your garage? One solution for extra income is to rent out your space to a friend or coworker. We have had several guests that have utilized this method at some point on their financial journey to increase their gap number. When I bought my first home, another teacher/coach from my school rented my secondary bedroom for $500 per month for two years. During those two years of house hacking, I used the rent money to cash flow my master's degree. Obtaining the master's degree gave me a 10% raise.

In 2021, my wife and I moved into our current primary residence. I was so excited to have a small studio apartment above our detached two and a half car garage. In my mind, this room above the garage was going to be the ultimate man cave. My wife had other intentions. She strongly suggested that we should house hack and rent it to traveling nurses via Furnished Finder (a direct booking service for traveling professionals). I was reluctant in the beginning, but this house hack has produced more income each month than our monthly mortgage payment for the last 18 months. Turns out, she was right... as usual.

As this book is being published, the max an individual can contribute to an IRA is $6,500 per year. We don't do basements near the beaches of North Carolina, but we've had multiple guests house hack and rent out a spare room or their finished basement. Maybe a fellow teacher could essentially fund your retirement for you as a roommate? We have met other teachers who rent multiple rooms out in their home and essentially cut their living expenses to zero.

SHORT-TERM & LONG-TERM RENTAL REAL ESTATE

Investing in real estate is a great idea, and there might not be a more lucrative return on your real estate investments than turning them into short-term or long-term rentals. Do you live near a college, big city, military base, airport, hospital, the beach, the mountains, or some other tourist attraction? People like experiencing a stay that goes beyond your ordinary hotel. This is not necessarily easy money as being a short-term rental manager puts you in the hospitality business. The good news is that we are teachers. We are accustomed to putting out fires (hopefully, not literal fires) and dealing with the public. Yes, it will take work, but the income that can be earned through short-term rentals has the potential to increase your gap number by a large sum of money. In 2020 and 2021, we converted two long-term rental units into short-term rentals. The long-term rentals were renting for $950 (each) but are now netting approximately $1850 (each) per month as short-term rentals. Long-term rentals are great too. They require less work and are a great alternative if your market doesn't lend itself to the short-term rental business. We will have more on rental real estate in Chapter Twelve.

LOOKING FOR YOUR WILD CARD

It is the FIT Position that good fortune will often present itself and can be seized by someone looking for it. A Wildcard is any opportunity that is presented that can benefit someone financially in a way that was totally unexpected. Keep your eyes and ears open. You never know when fate will roll in with just the thing that you need to springboard you ahead on the journey toward financial independence. More to come on this under the third imperative.

BE INTENTIONAL WITH EXTRA INCOME

The key to making a second job, side hustle, etc. work for you is to be disciplined with the money made. The extra time and effort will be well worth it if you can get ahead financially, but if you allow yourself to use the extra money for a more expensive lifestyle, you will have accomplished no good. The extra money that you earn should be used to either pay off debt, fully fund your savings account, or be used to purchase assets such as shares in an index fund or real estate. It should not be spent on extra trips to the local buffet or watering hole.

BOTTOM LINE

Building wealth is dependent upon a healthy gap number. Remember, increasing the amount of your monthly gap number is done in three ways: spending less money, paying off debt, and making more money.

CHAPTER SEVEN ACTION STEPS

1. Max out your earning potential by developing a plan to get your master's degree and/or National Board Certification (if the state that you live in pays extra for these).

2. Max out your earning potential by taking on some paid duties in your school.

3. Explore the possibility of taking on a part-time job for a specific purpose such as paying off debt, fully funding your savings account, or earning a specific level of money to invest.

4. Do you have a skill set that you could use to start a side-hustle? Could you go back to school and learn a trade to help in this endeavor? Explore this option to see if it might be right for you.

5. Look for jobs teaching in a foreign country. A few years could change everything.

6. House-Hacking. Renting a room can be a financial game-changer.

7. Consider the short-term or long-term rental game.

8. Be intentional with all extra money made. What supplements or stipends are you already receiving? How are these lump sums being used? Use them to build wealth.

CHAPTER EIGHT
THE APATHETIC INVESTOR

"I can't pick winning individual stocks,
and neither can you."
~JL Collins

If you are like I was and know nothing about investing, and maybe you don't even care to know much about it, don't let the information in the next few chapters discourage you. Before we started recording the *Financially Independent Teachers Podcast*, I knew some of the language associated with investing, but I had no personal experience with it. Honestly, I didn't have enough confidence to start investing on my own, and I didn't have enough money to work with a financial advisor. To make matters worse, I was embarrassed to ask anyone what I didn't know about investing. Had it not been for Dave asking me to tag along on this journey, I probably would never have gotten started. As mentioned, I was the affable loser on the show from day one. People expected me to ask the questions that others would be too embarrassed to ask. I'll never forget the episode where I decided that I would start investing.

I'm going to tell you in just a few words all that you really need to know to build a nest egg that will change your family tree. Speaking of trees... did you know it takes the average orange seed 8-15 years to grow into an orange producing tree? Nothing earth shattering, but you can't plant a seed and give up hope for a harvest after just a few years of not seeing significant progress. Investing can be complicated, or it can be simple. Either way, you will need the patience of Job. I like simple things because I am a simple person. If you are a like me, here it is:

I don't want to invest in something that I don't know much about. That is why I invest in a total US stock market index fund. I don't understand much, but I do understand what the American stock market is, and if I can buy shares in an index fund that has almost every publicly traded company in it, then that is what I am going to do. Some companies will do well, some won't. Over the course of decades, investing in a fund like this has historically returned an "average" of 8%-10%.

You don't have to pick winners and losers in the stock market. Not even the "experts" are good at that. Investing in a total American market index fund gives you ownership of a small piece of thousands of US companies. Invest in the entire American stock market for the win. What do you have to lose? If the entire American market tanks, you'll lose your money, but who cares? At that point we're all screwed anyway.

Go to Vanguard and open a Roth IRA. Just follow the steps to open the Roth IRA. If you have any questions during the process, call the helpline. They are friendly and informational. You are a middle-income earner. You want to use Vanguard and you want a Roth IRA. Connect your checking account with your Vanguard account, transfer some money over, and you are ready to invest.

If you want to invest in the total American stock market, invest in a total stock market index fund.

Automate it. Every month, allocate as much as you can, set it, and forget it. Check it once a year. You won't be accessing this account until you are 59.5 years old. When the market is down, shares will be on sale. When the market is up, the shares you own will be worth more than you paid for them.

You can currently invest $6,500 ($7,500 if 50+) in your Roth IRA per year. Automate $500 per month, and then when you do your one time per year check, throw another $500 in there. That's it. You are maxing out your Roth IRA and you are a big-time investor.

When investing in a Roth IRA, the gains in your account grow tax free.

If you have a spouse, both of you can have a Roth IRA and both of you can max it out. $6,500 for you and another $6,500 for your spouse.

That's it. That's all that you must know. No need to worry about investing in anything from your school or district. Set a goal to max out your Roth IRA, and if you are married, encourage your spouse to do the same. If you can do this, your future self will give you a hearty "thank you" for the wealth you've built.

CASE STUDY: 35 YEAR VETERAN TEACHER

Hundreds of thousands of educators will be riding off into the sunset and entering retirement this summer. Although it is fun to dream about the "what-ifs" of our future investments, let's look back at the actual stock market performance of a teacher hired in the summer of 1988. The teacher in our case study was very fortunate to have a mentor educator who bullied them into investing $150 per month, every month when they were first hired. Even as their income grew with advanced degrees and other raises, this teacher never increased their investments beyond their original automated $150 per month. As they head into retirement, how much would this teacher have in their investment accounts after 35 years? Since 1988, the stock market has produced a 10% rate of return. The teacher's investment of $150 per month (every month) would give them approximately a $487,000 nest egg as they transition into retirement. Imagine if they had invested their monthly car payments, too? If you have time on your side, it is amazing what $150 per month can turn into.

If you want to know more about stock market investing, read on to Chapter Nine (Investment Tax Shelters) and Chapter Ten (Stock Market Investing). If not, skip to Chapter Eleven (Your Primary Residence)

The numbers in this book represent the current IRS rules as of 2023. Past performance doesn't guarantee future results.

CHAPTER EIGHT ACTION STEPS

1. Open a Roth IRA with Vanguard.

2. Start contributing to your Roth IRA and invest in a total American market index fund.

3. Make your investments automatic so you never have to remember to do it on your own.

4. Be patient and let compound interest do its thing.

5. As you get raises and pay off debt, increase your contributions until you are maxing out your Roth IRA.

CHAPTER NINE
INVESTMENT
TAX SHELTERS

*"Investors need to understand not only the magic of
compounding long-term returns,
but the tyranny of compounding costs;
costs that ultimately overwhelm the magic."*
~Jack Bogle

For many, investing is a topic in personal finance that is shrouded in mystery. Most teachers understand the concept of investing but lack the know-how and confidence to get started. Brandon mentioned in the previous chapter that he didn't know much about investing until recently. I am not too far ahead of him as I knew nothing about investing until I crossed the age of 30. Many teachers and middle-income earners have been led astray by the promise of riches in the day-trading game. Apps such as Robin Hood have come along, and they offer fool's gold to the masses, and they are partying like it's 1849. And going broke like it's 1849. Investing is not a get rich quick scheme. Building wealth by investing requires time, constant pressure, patience, and the guts to take the hits as the market fluctuates daily. The type of stock market investing that is FIT approved is simple, but it is not easy. The stock market, over time, has always grown. In the short term it is volatile, but over time, the stock market has always grown.

As you invest your money on a regular basis, the interest

compounds every year, and as the years go by, you will notice significant growth. There's a reason why Einstein stated, "Compound interest is the eighth wonder of the world." We can't emphasize enough the power of starting early. Based on historical returns, an individual with $25,000 invested in the stock market by the age of 25 would likely be a net-worth millionaire by the age of 65, without ever investing another penny. That is the magic of compound interest. We call this the FIT "25k by 25 Rule". If you are young, the best thing you have on your side is Father Time, but you must be fearless.

Initial Investment	Years	Rate of Return	Growth	Total
$25,000	40	10%	$1,317,516	$1,342,516

We don't believe anyone should be able to graduate from high school without understanding the concept of the FIT "25k by 25 Rule." If you are already 25+ years old and haven't accomplished the FIT 25k by 25 Rule, share this information with your younger colleagues, friends, and family. Brandon was 43 years old when he started investing in the stock market. He doesn't have the kind of time on his side that he did when he was 22-years old, but he still has 20-25 years left before he plans to retire. That is enough time for compound interest to work a little magic. Luckily, compound interest doesn't retire when you do. It will continue to go to work, even after you exit the workforce.

GOVERNMENT TAX SHELTERS

How would you like to make money and pay no taxes on your earnings? Believe it or not, you can do this and not go to jail. The government has given us several tax shelters by which we can invest our money. Properly taking advantage of these tax shelters allows you to legally not pay the IRS. Ready for some good news? Teachers usually have multiple tax shelters available to them. There is a great deal here to unpack, but we are going to do our best to keep it simple. You can think of a "tax shelter" as something like a bucket, or a place to fill up or store your money.

The government makes the rules and the numbers listed below can and will change in the future.

The following are a handful of major tax shelters that will help you build wealth:

1. Individual Retirement Account/Arrangement (IRA): this type of account is available to almost anyone who has earned income. One can contribute $6,500 ($7,500 if age 50 or older) per year to this account. If you are married, both you and your spouse can contribute to their own IRA ($13,000-$15,00 total per year). If you are married to a spouse who stays at home, the spouse does not need to have "earned" income to contribute to an IRA (if you file taxes jointly). If you are a high-income earner or married to one, you could make too much money to qualify for an IRA. Yes, there are ways around this rule but that is for another book.

The two types of IRA's that impact teachers and middle-income earners most are **Roth** and **Traditional**. The main difference? You can get the tax break now (Traditional) or get the tax break later (Roth). Both above-mentioned IRA's have their own benefits. We will discuss some of the differences between a Roth and a Traditional IRA later in this chapter.

For many middle-income earners, opening an IRA and maxing it out each year will be all you need on your investing journey, but we understand there are some unicorms out there who will move beyond this. In any event, maxing your IRA is a non-negotiable and a major financial feat.

2. 457(b): You can invest up to $22,500 ($30,000 if age 50 or older) into your 457(b) and you can withdraw your money from this account at any time **once separated from your employer.** You do not have to wait until a specific age to access it. Not all teachers will have access to a 457(b). This shelter comes through your employer, so you are limited to the investment options provided through your employer. It is important to note the Roth 457(b) does not grant early access like the traditional 457(b).

3. 403(b) & 401(k): these accounts have the same contribution limits as the 457(b), but you cannot make withdrawals until you are 59.5 (unless you retire between ages 55-59.5). You can invest $22,500 ($30,000 for those age 50 or older) per year. As a teacher, you will likely have access to one of these through your employer. Like the 457(b), your investment options are limited to what is offered through your employer.

*457(b), 403(b), and 401(k) represent the place in the tax code where these provisions are located.**

MORE ON ROTH V. TRADITIONAL

A "Roth" tax shelter means that the money that you are investing has already been taxed and will therefore grow tax free. As an example, if you've contributed $100,000 into your Roth IRA and it's now worth $500,000, the magic of compound interest has grown your account by $400,000. Once you reach the age of 59.5, you can withdraw all the money in your Roth IRA, without paying taxes on any of that $500,000. Who doesn't love tax free gains?

On the other hand, the "traditional" option grants the tax break on the front end. For example, if you gross $50,000 a year, and you contribute $10,000 to your traditional 457(b), your taxable income would be $40,000 instead of $50,000. This approach will reduce your current tax burden. However, if your money grows and is worth $1,000,000 one day, Uncle Sam will come calling. You will have to pay taxes on your future withdrawals.

For most teachers, the Roth option is always better if it is available. There is typically not a compelling reason for a middle-income earner to reduce their taxable income and sacrifice the tax-free growth of the Roth option. If you have a high-income earning spouse, you can always do a mixture of both.

THE FEE EFFECT

Beware of the sharply dressed individual who will attempt to set up a seemingly harmless meeting over pizza and soda during your planning period. When investing in your workplace retirement accounts, be aware of the fees that are associated with these accounts. The 403(b) is infamously known for having extremely high fees.

What are investment fees? Investment fees are used to pay the managers of your investment account. Fees cover product trading, marketing, expense ratios, etc. Based on historical returns, a one-time $10,000 investment into an account with a 0.04% fee will grow to approximately $446,000 in 40 years. On the flip side, the same $10,000 invested into an account with a 2.0% fee would end up being $217,000. We recently worked with a client who did not realize they were paying 1.5% in fees through their district provided vendor. Do you know how much you are paying in fees? 1% or 2% doesn't seem like much in the here and now but it could cost you tens of thousands down the road.

Many states and local districts offer terrible investment products. For this reason, we recommend that you look at the grade your state and local school district has been given by Dan Otter at his 403(b)wise website: www.403bwise.com. Dan has done some outstanding work and his website is a wonderful resource for anyone that wants to understand more about personal finances and investing. If the vendors available to you are bad, you need to know that before you start contributing. Many have had to learn by being burned and we don't want that to happen to you.

CATCH-UP CONTRIBUTIONS

When you are young, there are some very important milestone birthdays to look forward to. We have good news, 21 isn't the last birthday to anticipate. Once you turn 50, the IRS will allow what they call "catch-up contributions" to your investment tax shelters. Catch-up contributions enable the investor to put more money into your investment shelters. Currently (2023), the IRS will allow an individual to contribute $6,500 (per year) into an IRA. However, if you are 50 or above, you can contribute $7,500 (per year). When it comes to other tax shelters like the 401(k),403(b) and 457(b), turning 50 will allow you to add an additional $7,500 to each bucket. A 40-year-old can "only" contribute $22,500 to a 401(k) but your 55-year-old teacher friend down the hall can contribute $30,000. Who says the IRS can't be nice? Take advantage of these IRS rules and play catch-up. After all, most of us were never taught money skills growing up and likely missed out on many years of investing. It could be worth it to extend your career by a few years to take advantage of catching up. Once you quit or retire, you won't be able to contribute to the 401(k), 403(b), or the 457(b).

THE FIT POSITION OF INVESTING
(ORDER OF INVESTING OPERATIONS)

We are often asked to rank/order the available tax shelters for people. After over 100 hours of conversations with teachers winning with money and financial authors and experts, we have come up with the following answer:

Important Note ...Not all of your employer accounts are created equal, the fees and options available to you could change the order of investing operations.

1. **Employer Match:** In the rare event that you work for a school district that will match your contributions or you have a spouse who has a matching contribution, the employer match will be the first place that you will want to invest your money. You will be limited to the company investment options provided, but even if you aren't a fan of the options, it is rarely a good idea to turn down the free money from the employer match.

2. **Roth IRA:** Most teachers will not have a matching option (spouse might). For most, a Roth IRA (tax free growth) is what we recommend as your first choice. Many teachers will be unable to invest more than the $6,500 per year, so the Roth IRA could be the only shelter needed. This will not be done through your employer, and you can open one up with Vanguard online. There are other respected platforms like Charles Schwab, M1 Finance and Fidelity, but most of our guests use Vanguard.

STOP! If you are single and have less than $6,500 per year to invest, the Roth IRA is all you need (or if you are married *with less than $13,000 per year to invest) we give you per-mission to skip ahead to* **HOW THESE TAX SHELTERS WORK.** *If your GAP number increases beyond the Roth IRA, be a lifelong learner and come back to steps 3-6.*

3. **457(b):** The next shelter we recommend is the 457(b) due to it affording the ability to make withdrawals once separated from your employer. If you wanted to retire at age 50, for example, your 457(b) could act as a bridge to get you to 59.5 years of age when you can access the growth in other tax shelters. You may or may not have access to a 457(b), but if you do, it's your next best option.

4. **401(k) or 403(b):** Then comes the 403(b) or 401(k). You will more than likely have access to one of these through your employer. You will be limited to the investment options pro-vided through work so beware of high fees.

5. **HSA:** If you have a high deductible health insurance plan (HDHP), then you might have access to a Health Savings Account. The HSA option could move up to #2 or #3 on this list if you have one available to you. The magic of the HSA is its "triple tax advantage." HSA's come with three main tax benefits: You can contribute to them on a pretax or tax-deduct-ible basis, and your savings grow free of taxes over time. You can also make tax-free withdrawals to cover qualified medical expenses.

6. **Brokerage Account:** If you are interested in more flexibility to gain access to your investments without the handcuffs of an age limit, one can also utilize a brokerage account and invest with-out tax benefits. Remember, personal finance is personal. Some might move this up on their list and that is understandable, especially if you don't want any age restrictions on your invest-ments. You will do this on your own via Vanguard, Fidelity, or whichever brokerage firm you are comfortable with. You don't need a financial planner to do this.

HOW THESE TAX SHELTERS WORK

These tax shelters are exactly what they sound like in that you place money in them, and the money will just sit there until it is invested. More than one person has made the mistake of opening a Roth IRA, for example, and putting money into that Roth IRA every month without investing it and wondered why the money was not growing. An IRA is not an investment; it is a bucket to store your investments in. You still must transfer money into it and purchase investments to go inside the bucket.

Step 1) open an account.

Step 2) put money in the account.

Step 3) purchase shares and start investing.

529 PLANS

If you have children, and if you think that it is your responsibility to pay for them to go to college, you might consider a 529 plan. The 529 is an investment tax shelter created by the government to help parents pay for the college education of their children. Recently, it has even expanded to K-12 education as well. We have discovered that there are different schools of thought on this.

Some of our guests believe that tasking their children with the responsibility of paying for their own college education builds character. FIT podcast guest and Ramsey Personality, Kristina Ellis is a great example of this. She wrote a book detailing how she earned thousands of dollars in scholarships. Her mother told her prior to her Ninth-grade year that she would have to find a way to pay for college. She in turn worked hard and found a way to not only pay for her bachelor's degree, but also her master's degree, and did so without taking out a loan.

On the other hand, some parents firmly believe that paying for their child's college education is their responsibility. Even if that is your philosophy, the FIT Position is to first save for your retirement. Then save for their education. Why? Because parents that break the bank on their kid's education and do not take care of their own retirement become burdens to their kids in their old age. I was very fortunate to have my family pay for my undergraduate degree. Graduating with no student loan debt was a wild card that accelerated me on my path to financial independence. The 529 plan or any other educational savings strategy must come after the steps required to establish yourself financially have been taken. Recent rule changes to the 529 make it a more favorable account as funds that are unused for college can be rolled into a Roth IRA starting in 2024. We encourage parents to inform their loved ones if they have a 529, this makes for a great birthday or Christmas gift.

BRIDGE ACCOUNTS

Many teachers can retire much earlier than the average American worker. Bridge accounts, as the name suggests, bridge the gap for a person who no longer has earned income but wants access to their investment accounts without prompting any early withdrawal penalties.

I will be able to retire as a North Carolina teacher and collect my pension starting at age 50; however, I will not be able to access my 401(k), 403(b), or Roth IRA (growth) investments until age 59.5, without penalty or other financial gymnastics. Banking on my pension alone at the age of 50 will likely not be enough for my wife and I to live off of. If I can't access the 401(k)/403(b)/IRA until 59.5 and social security isn't an option until 62, I might need another form of income to bridge myself to those later dates. Fortunately, there are many ways to have access to funds beyond your pension, even if you retire early.

STRATEGIES FOR "BRIDGING" YOUR WAY TO 59.5

457(b): We love the 457(b) because it gives a teacher access to a bridge account, if needed. As soon as a teacher **separates service** with their employer, they have access (penalty free) to their 457(b) investments, regardless of age.

Brokerage Account: An investment account that has zero tax benefits. You can invest in low-cost index funds in your broker-age accounts virtually free and be in complete control of these investments, regardless of your employment status. This account is not tied at all to your place of employment, and there are no limits to how much you can invest in your brokerage account each year. There are no penalties for accessing your money and cashing out your investments. Some prefer to have this flexibility and not worry about the lack of tax advantages.

Roth IRA: Again, we are not fans of tapping into investments early, but the Roth IRA gives flexibility to the investor to access their contributions penalty free at any time. This makes the Roth IRA a de facto savings account. What can't be touched? The growth of the investments in the Roth IRA.

Rule of 55: Plot twist! If you stop teaching in your district after age 55 but before age 59.5, the IRS allows you to access your invest-ments without penalty. This only applies to accessing funds from your current employer (the one you retire from), previous contribu-tions from old districts wouldn't qualify for the "Rule of 55." For instance, if you are considering retiring at 54, it might be worth it to work one more year and grant yourself early access to your investments without a penalty.

Back to the Workforce: If you are retiring in your early to mid-50s, you certainly have the skill set, connections, and the energy (potentially) to get back in the workforce. In North Carolina, you can come back and work for the state in the form of being a substitute or even part time teacher after you've been retired for six months. I know many North Carolina teachers who net more money each month in retirement by collecting their pension and teaching a half day than they did working full-time. Some teachers will hop across state lines and immediately make top of the pay scale money while collecting a pension from the state they retired from. Some retired teachers continue their careers in a private school where they can draw their pension and receive full teacher pay. Private schools often pay less than the public school system, but it is a nice supplement to the pension.

You could even choose to get out of education all together and start a new path.

Rental Real Estate: We will talk more about this in Chapter Twelve, but passive real estate income can replace your salary until you have access to your retirement accounts.

CHAPTER NINE ACTION STEPS

1. Based on your budget, check your gap number to determine how many investment buckets you could fill up.

2. Identify what tax shelters are available to you in your district and whether you have access to an employer match. Then use the FIT Position order of operations to decide which shelters you will utilize and in what order.

3. Go to www.403bwise.com and look up the grade that your state and district have received. If there is no grade available, email Dan Otter about having your district assessed. They are currently trying to assess every district in America.

4. Look to see what the expense ratios (fees) of your workplace investment options are. Beware of high fees.

5. Open the account. Put money into the account. Purchase investment products within your investment bucket.

6. Make it automatic. Just like your Netflix bill each month, you don't want to have to remember to make a payment/contribution. Set your investing to recurring and auto transactions so you are on autopilot, no matter how busy life gets.

CHAPTER TEN
STOCK MARKET INVESTING

"Investing should be more like watching paint dry or watching grass grow. If you want excitement, take $800 and go to Las Vegas."
~Paul Samuelson

Now that we are aware of the tax shelters available, the basic rules associated with each, and understand the order of operations for selecting the shelters that are best for us... now what? We believe it is important to start investing as early as possible to take advantage of the magic of compound interest and to develop the habit of investing. Many pundits say you should not start investing until you are debt free. We disagree. Based on conversations with many middle-income earners, most never started investing because they were intimidated by the process. Opening the account and automating your investment is crucial. We do believe that before you start investing **large sums** of money, you should be executing a budget with a high degree of success, be debt free, and have a fully funded savings account.

Once you reach this step, all you must do is increase your contributions. The fear of opening the account and getting started was accomplished long before. Investing can be a scary proposition. Most are intimidated because they don't think that they know enough to execute a plan without the help of a financial professional. That is a reasonable fear. You should never invest in anything that you don't fully understand. For this reason, we are big fans of index funds. They are easy to understand and come highly recommended.

HOW DOES THE STOCK MARKET WORK?

When you put money into the stock market, you are exchanging your money for "shares" of a publicly traded company or multiple companies. In turn, companies use the money raised by selling shares to grow and expand their business. As the business grows, the company's stock increases in value. In the mid-80s, Michael Jordan signed a marketing deal with Nike. In 1985, one share of Nike stock was worth 0.14. At the time of writing this book, one share of Nike stock sells for $124. What does that mean? An individual who invested $1,000 in Nike stock in 1985 would have been able to purchase 7,142 shares of Nike at that time. Today, those 7,142 shares of Nike are worth $885,000! Nike has turned out to be a great investment... Blockbuster Video, Sears, Toys "R" Us... not so much. Investing in one individual company or a "single stock" is not something that we recommend. As we dive deeper into this chapter, we will teach you about a more diverse type of investment called an index fund. While the market fluctuates daily, it is historically "up" approximately seven out of every ten years. Remember, the tortoise always beats the hare. Stock market investing is viewed as a long-term play, not a get-rich-quick scheme, and you don't have to be an "expert" to succeed.

MORE ON OPENING AN INVESTMENT ACCOUNT

If you are like most teachers, the first (and potentially only) tax shelter that you will be using is the Roth IRA. **You will not be opening your Roth IRA through your employer.** Don't let this intimidate you. You can do this on your own. If you get confused, you can simply call the helpline and they will help you with your questions. We firmly believe in opening the Roth IRA, even if you are in debt. The most difficult part is often getting the courage to open the account and start automating contributions. There are three steps that you need to follow:

FIRST: OPEN AN ACCOUNT

The FIT Position is to open your Roth IRA with Vanguard for three major reasons:

1. The moment you open your Roth IRA with Vanguard, you are a part owner of Vanguard.

2. Their helpline is outstanding. If you call with a question, you will get someone competent on the other end of the phone.

3. Vanguard investment products are some of the best available.

You just cannot go wrong with Vanguard.

Opening a Vanguard account could not be easier. You simply go to Vanguard's website, follow the directions to open a Roth IRA, and then follow the directions to link your primary checking account to your Roth IRA. It's that simple. If you have any problems call the helpline where a professional will take your call and guide you through the process.

SECOND: PUT MONEY INTO YOUR ROTH IRA ACCOUNT

Once your checking account is linked, you will be able to transfer money into your Roth IRA from your checking account. Placing money into your Roth IRA account is not the same thing as investing it. Once you transfer the money into your account, it is just sitting there in a settlement fund (like savings) waiting to be invested. You still need to select investments to go into the bucket.

THIRD: START INVESTING YOUR CONTRIBUTIONS

At Financially Independent Teachers, we are not certified financial planners; however, we do have a recommendation for investing. Our investing values line up with author and friend of the show, JL Collins. We follow the JL Collins approach that he outlines in his book, *The Simple Path to Wealth*. Do yourself a favor and read his book. In case you forgot, JL wrote the amazing foreword to *The FIT Position*.

JL Collins recommends Vanguard, and he recommends the Vanguard total stock market index fund (VTSAX). With JL's approach, you don't have to stress over picking individual companies.

HERE ARE A FEW THINGS THAT YOU SHOULD KNOW ABOUT INVESTING IN INDEX FUNDS:

1. Index funds usually follow one of the major indexes used to measure the performance of the stock market. For example, you can buy shares in an S&P 500 index fund. This fund will contain within it shares of every company in the S&P 500. The S&P 500 is composed of the 500 most successful publicly traded US companies. If you own an S&P 500 fund, you are part owner of Tesla, Google, Apple, Meta, Home Depot, Walmart and 494 other highly successful companies. One fascinating thing about the S&P 500, and all other index funds, is that they are "self-cleansing." If a company is doing poorly, it could drop out of the S&P 500 and a new and up and coming company will replace it. The best part? This is automatically done for you, and there is no need for an active manager that will charge you a ridiculous amount in fees.

2. Total market index funds allow you to own stock in virtually every company being traded on the market. For a total market index fund to fail, the whole market would have to collapse... in which case we are all doomed anyway. Buying a total market fund automatically diversifies your portfolio and is the investment product that JL Collins recommends in his book *The Simple Path to Wealth*. Even when investing in a total US market index fund or the S&P 500, these companies do business all over the world. In a sense, this also gives you international exposure.

3. Index funds and mutual funds are often mistaken as the same investment product because they are both very diverse. The main difference between a mutual fund and an index fund is that mutual funds are actively managed by a professional money manager. For this reason, there are higher fees associated with mutual funds. The dirty little secret about mutual funds is that 87% of them do not outperform the total market index. If you can find a mutual fund that has been around for over ten years, consistently outperforms the total market index, and

has a rate of return of more than 12% (rendering the fees associated with the fund palatable), consider investing in a mutual fund. On the other hand, if you do not want to go searching for the proverbial "needle in a haystack," start buying shares in a total market index fund or an S&P 500 index, automate it, and forget about it. This is JL Collins' approach, and it is the one that we have adopted, as well as most of the guests that have appeared on our show.

4. Automate your contributions and investments and do not give it another thought. It is very simple to have money electronically transferred from your checking account to your investment accounts. When your investment is set to automatic, you never have to remember to invest again. Do not check it every day. On a day-to-day basis the market is volatile. Over time, the stock market has always grown. Those that check it every day or even weekly usually find the temptation to sell when the market is in a downturn difficult to resist. Selling out of fear is always a bad idea. Let it ride. Be fearless.

TIME HORIZON

When the market is down, shares are on sale. Volatility is your friend. Your money will buy more shares when the market is down, and when the market rises again, those shares that you bought will be worth much more than you paid for them. You should not try to time the market. That is a fool's game. Time IN the market is more important than TIMING the market. The longer time horizon you must invest, the better. Consistently invest in quality total market index funds and with the passing of each decade your money will grow faster and faster. In 2008, the S&P 500 lost 38% of its value and took two years to recover. From 2010-2020, the S&P averaged an annualized 12% return. It just takes time and pressure.

JL was our guest for episode #69 and episode #107 on our podcast. We would strongly encourage you to listen to both of those episodes.

CHAPTER TEN ACTION STEPS

1. Check to see if you have an employer match available to you (unlikely). If you do, sign up and take advantage of it. If you are married, see if your spouse has a match as well. Don't pass on FREE money.

2. Open a Roth IRA and start transferring money from your checking account to your Roth IRA. Set it up on auto draft. Don't forget to actually invest the money.

3. No matter your situation, start investing NOW to develop the habit and overcome fear of the unknown. Investing $20 a month is better than nothing. You can always increase later.

4. Consider the three items mentioned that should be completed before heavily investing. Execute a budget, be debt free, and have a fully funded emergency savings account.

5. If you have money left over to invest after the Roth IRA, consider utilizing a workplace tax shelter like a 457(b), 401(k), or 403(b). Check the fees.

6. If you can invest in a tax shelter offered through your employer, set that up with the appropriate person in your district's central office, and start automating your contributions.

7. Read the *Simple Path to Wealth*, by JL Collins

CHAPTER ELEVEN
YOUR PRIMARY HOME

"Whether you rent or buy,
you pay for the home you occupy."
~Rick Osborne

Most who have appeared on our podcast have said that buying a primary residence is a key component to living the "American Dream." The middle-income earner's primary residence is one of the most important financial decisions of their lifetime, and retirement can happen sooner and be happier once it is paid off. While there are plenty of arguments on the role homeownership plays in building wealth, most of our guests who are winning with money are homeowners. To be fair, the lion's share of our guests live in the Midwest or Southeast. Buying a home is important but should not be done before you are ready. Prior to buying a home, we recommend executing a budget with a reasonably high degree of success, be debt free, or mostly debt free, and have a fully funded savings account. The push-back on this is, "most people don't have these things in place prior to buying a home." We hate to point out the obvious, but most people are broke and make unwise decisions when it comes to money.

DO I NEED AN AGENT? HOW MUCH DOES IT COST?

When buying a home, you need a good real estate agent. A quality real estate agent can be a tremendous help and resource. A bad one can make your life miserable. Keep in mind that when "hiring" an agent, they work for you for free. It doesn't cost a penny to have an agent find you the home of your dreams. The agent only gets paid if you buy a house. Guess what? The commission is paid by the seller of the home, not you (the buyer).

LOAN PRE-QUALIFICATION

Some people have champagne taste on a beer budget. As fun as it is to dream of homeownership on Zillow, be careful falling in love with a house you cannot afford. My wife is a real estate agent, and she will not take a client out until they have a pre-approval letter from a lender. The reason? Psychologically, it is hard to go backwards. If you are approved by the lender for $300,000 but find yourself looking at homes above that price point, you are wasting your time and the agents. Everyone loves what they can't afford. It doesn't cost any money to see if you pre-qualify, so if you are legitimately interested in buying a home, we recommend getting one early in the process. The bank will be looking at your debt-to-income ratio and your credit score. **BEWARE! Many banks will pre-qualify you for more than you can afford. Just because a bank says you CAN doesn't mean you SHOULD.**

TAKING OUT A MORTGAGE

Shop around for the right kind of loan that suits your needs. You need to know exactly what you are looking for in a home and know your limitations. If you could buy a fixer-upper at a great price, can you successfully do most of the work yourself? If not, consider the cost that you will incur hiring others to do the work. The purchase of a primary residence is a huge investment for a middle-income earner. Spend some time thinking about what you really want and what you can afford.

As far as financing is concerned, consider a 15-year mortgage, if possible. If the monthly payment on a 15-year mortgage is too high, it is important to keep in mind that a 30-year mortgage can always be paid off early. You can make extra (principal only) payments to shorten the life of the loan. Many people with good intentions have failed to shorten their 30-year mortgage with extra payments, but a 15-year loan gives you a home that is paid off in, well, 15 years. As an example, paying off a mortgage of $250,000 in 15 years will save a homeowner over $200,000 in interest (compared to a 30-year mortgage). On the flip side, a 30-year mortgage provides some nice flexibility to have a smaller monthly payment in case disaster strikes. Don't bite off more than you can chew. The sooner you can pay off a primary residence, the sooner you can free up that mortgage payment to continue building wealth.

Last, we recommend a fixed rate on your mortgage. With a fixed rate, the bank can't raise your interest rate over time. Beware of variable interest rates. In any event, we don't recommend your mortgage being more than 30% of your monthly take home pay... and that is probably too much.

TYPES OF LOANS

1. **USDA Loan:** very little down payment (possibly none) in more rural areas. You'd be surprised at what classifies as rural. This helps you get into a home without draining your savings account.

2. **FHA Loan:** a mortgage insured by the government and potentially only 3.5% down needed. Another way to get into a home with very little money upfront.

3. **Conventional Loan:** not backed by the government, usually requiring 20% down by a bank or private lender.

4. **VA Loan:** Have you or a spouse ever served in the US military? If so, you might qualify for a VA loan. A VA loan is a mortgage guaranteed by the United States Department of Veteran Affairs. The biggest benefit of a VA loan? The borrower can purchase a home with no money down (100% financing).

In some cases, not putting down 20% could require the buyer to purchase Private Mortgage Insurance. This usually adds an extra $100 per month to your payment and is essentially foreclosure insurance. You can eventually drop PMI, but it should be avoided if possible.

WHAT ABOUT INSURANCE?

Shop around for the best rates when purchasing a home. There is something to be said for having all your insurance needs serviced in one place. All of Brandon's different insurance policies are housed in one place and managed by one agent. He likes knowing that when he texts or calls his agent that he will get a response in a reasonable amount of time. You can also get discounts when you bundle your insurance with one company. Whether the rate is most important to you or the company that you deal with is most important, the big thing is that you take charge of your insurance needs.

HOME INSPECTION

Before you close on the home, it is worth the few hundred-dollar investment to get a home inspection. A home inspection could save you potential headaches and tens of thousands of dollars in unforeseen repairs. If the home inspection is bad enough, it can be used as a negotiation tool with sellers to fix the problems or lower the purchase price.

BUYING YOUNG

If you are in college and are reading this book, then you are in the perfect position to build wealth and become a net-worth millionaire long before retirement age. As a young teacher, you can potentially buy a home in your mid-20s and have it paid off by your mid-40s or early 50s. The life of a 30-year mortgage (depending on your interest rate) is cut down by approximately seven to eight years by simply making one extra principal payment per year. Not having a mortgage in your mid-40s or early 50s frees up a great deal of money to invest in the stock market or purchase more real estate.

At the time of the writing of this book, the real estate market in the US has gone wild. Buying young in your area might seem unrealistic. In our low cost of living area in Eastern NC, two of Dave's former students (both single NC educators) purchased homes before the age of 25 and each took out a 15-year mortgage.

Because of the sacrifice they are making with larger monthly payments in their 20s, these teachers will have their homes paid off before they reach the age of 41. Both did their own form of "house hacking" and lived at home their first few years teaching to save up enough money for a quality down payment.

Real estate is local and depending on which part of the country you live in, it might be feasible to buy. Buying a house might create a much longer commute than you want as you venture into a lower cost of living area. Owning a home can be very expensive, but so can renting. To be clear, there is a time and place for renting. Renters should not be shamed. Nonetheless, paying attention to how much you pay in rent over an extended period is something to consider. Proponents of renting would argue that it is a plus to not have to worry about mortgage, taxes, insurance, or home repairs. Of course, a landlord will likely make sure their tenant is covering all of these in the monthly rent price. Let's say that a teacher pays $1,000 in rent (every month) and stays in that location for a decade. Renting for the price tag of $12,000 per year (for a decade) turns into $120,000. How much of that $120,000 will the teacher get when they move out? If they are lucky, their $1,000 security deposit. We've come across colleagues who have rented for a decade or more, and for the same price as their monthly rent, they could have easily owned their own home. Just like stock market investing, the real estate market swings up and down. In the end, a home purchased in 2023 will likely be worth much more in 2050 than it was purchased originally. Even during times of high inflation, real estate allows individuals to ride the wave.

CHAPTER ELEVEN ACTION STEPS

1. Have a FIT Position budget in place that you have been successfully executing for several months.

2. Be debt free or mostly debt free.

3. Have a fully funded savings account.

4. Get a pre-approval letter from a lender for money that you can borrow for a home.

5. Find a good real-estate agent. Take your time in finding the right one.

6. Shop around for the right kind of loan from the right lender. Are you eligible for an FHA loan? A USDA loan? VA loan?

7. Doing business with your insurance agent for home insurance is a wonderful way to go if possible. I use the same company and the same agent for everything. You might be able to get better rates by shopping around, but I like working with the same agent for all my insurance needs.

8. Before closing, get a home inspection. It could save the day.

9. If you are renting, be aware of how much money you will be spending in rent per year to set a timetable for how long you want to remain in a rental. Remember the example of paying $1,000 a month for 10 years. You need to come to terms with how much money you are willing to spend on rent.

CHAPTER TWELVE
RENTAL REAL ESTATE

"Real estate investing, even on a very small scale, remains a tried and true means of building an individual's cash flow and wealth."
~Robert Kiyosaki

Real estate comes in many shapes and sizes. Whether it be renting out a room (house hacking), buying a duplex, or owning a single-family home, all have been discussed by guests on the podcast. Like the stock market, you must be fearless enough to navigate all the ups and downs that real estate offers. Real estate can be very complex, I highly recommend the *Bigger Pockets* podcast as well as their books if you want a more detailed explanation of rental real estate. Before I met my wife, I never imagined real estate would be much of a factor in my life. Today, real estate has become a passion of mine and is getting us closer and closer to financial independence. As we get into some of the basics of rental real estate, always remember that you make your money on the purchase of the property, not the sale. What does that mean? It simply means that you are buying "right." Finding an undervalued home or a property that has cosmetic issues will get you in at a lower price point compared to properties that are "show ready." Like the stock market, real estate will have its ups and downs. If you try to time the market, you might never get in. If the market turns south, hang on, buckle up and don't jump off the ride.

There are the three main ways to win with rental real estate.

They are;

1. **Cash Flow:** the income a property produces after all expenses have been paid
2. **Mortgage Principal Paydown:** at the outset of a home loan, most of your monthly payment will go to interest. As time moves on, more and more of your monthly payment goes to the principal, reducing the balance on your loan which will increase your home's equity.
3. **Appreciation:** the increase in value of a property over a period.

Cash Flow + Mortgage Principal Pay down + Appreciation = <u>Wealth Building</u>

HOW TO GET INTO RENTAL REAL ESTATE

There are several paths by which you might enter the rental game:

1. Paying off a home earlier in life.
2. Selling your primary home, downsizing, and using the profit on a rental property
3. Building additional living quarters on the property of your primary residence.
4. Purchasing a new primary residence and renting out your previous residence.
5. Parlaying an inheritance into a rental property.
6. Strategically building a team of investors to purchase rental properties.

CAN ONE MOVE CHANGE YOUR LIFE?

Can shifting your address and the four walls around you change your life forever? Yes! When considering moving, it is important to keep in mind that if a property has been your primary residence for two of the last five years, there is no capital gains tax upon the sale of the home. At the time of this book's release, an earner filing "single" can make up to $250,000 on the sale of their home tax free. A married couple filing "jointly" can make up to $500,000 on the sale of a house tax free.

As mentioned, when discussing flipping lifestyle creep, we lived in a neighborhood filled with teachers and other middle-income earners. Inspired by the Netflix film "Minimalism: A Documentary About the Important Things," we sold our 3,600 square foot home and walked away with $85,000 cash (TAX FREE). One move changed everything. Could you downsize and reduce your cost of living to increase your Gap Number?

Bigger Home = More Cleaning

Bigger Home = More Property Taxes + Insurance

Bigger Home = More Utility Costs

TEAM TEACHING

As middle-income earners with limited funds, getting in the game on your own might be difficult. There is a solution to that problem. We had one teacher guest on the FIT podcast who teamed up with three other teachers to get started in team real estate investing. The main advantage to forming a team is being able to divide the 20% down payment on a property between multiple people. In the case of our guest, instead of having to personally save up 20% for an investment property down payment, he and his team divide the 20% down payment four ways. By retirement, they are hoping to have 12 properties that are paid for, free and clear. At the end of their strategy, each teacher will own three properties outright. Long-term rentals are generally way more passive than short-term rentals.

To secure quality tenants, be a good landlord. In addition, secure background checks, credit checks, and proof of income when screening and trying to find the best tenants possible.

THE 1% RULE

When looking to purchase a rental property, consider the 1% rule. This rule isn't the end all be all, but it is a good measure to see if a piece of property is a "good deal." What is the 1% rule? The rule states that the monthly rental income should be 1% or more of the unit's purchase price. As an example, if you are speculating on purchasing a $200,000 property, the monthly rent it brings in needs to be at least $2,000 per month. In most cases, it isn't wise to buy a property that leaves you paying any part of the monthly mortgage. That is what the tenant is for. The rate of rent should cover your monthly payment.

THE MAGIC OF 1031

A rental real estate tool that is worth mentioning is tax code Section 1031, the provision in this section enables an individual to essentially "swap" or "trade" one piece of rental real estate property for another rental property. Remember, if you've lived in a property two out of the last five years, you can sell it and turn a profit without having to pay taxes. However, if your property hasn't been your primary residence for two of the last five years, you would have to pay capital gains tax on the income made from the sale. For example, imagine having an older rental that you know has lots of upcoming expenses. You could sell your old aging rental, take the profit, and use it to purchase a newer rental property, owing no taxes on the profit from the sale. **The key is you must use the proceeds to buy another RENTAL property.** You can't use it for your primary home. If you don't utilize the 1031 exchange, you will have to pay capital gains taxes on the sale of the rental property. Currently, there is no limit to how many times you can do this.

BONUS REAL ESTATE STRATEGY

You might also consider an alternative to the 529 plan (Chapter Eight) if you are interested in funding the higher education endeavors of your children. You could purchase rental property when your children are young, or before they are born, rent it out until they are of age, and then sell it. You could then take the profit from the sale and use it to pay for school. Essentially, your tenants are paying for the college education of your children over the course of time. If the home is paid off, you could use the cash flow to pay for college without having to sell.

SHORT TERM RENTALS

A short-term rental is generally considered to be a rental that is used for a stay that is less than 30 days. My wife and I have four short-term rental properties. One of our units is an ADU (Accessory Dwelling Unit) located on the site of our primary home. This detached apartment above our garage has been turned into an STR (short-term rental) and provides enough income to cover the monthly mortgage payment on our primary home. Some view real estate as "passive" income. If you think short term rentals are passive, you are mistaken. In the short-term rental game, your property must always be "show ready." This means the grass, landscaping, and general upkeep of the inside and outside of the property must be exquisite. Guests often leave online reviews, so you want to always make a good impression, or your business will suffer. The two major platforms for short-term rentals are Airbnb and VRBO. It isn't a good idea to rely solely on these companies to be the lifeline of your rental portfolio. Having a direct booking site or social media page will save money in fees and allow for repeat guests to book through you and cut out the middleman.

SHORT TERM RENTAL PROS

1. **Greater profit:** It isn't unusual for a short-term rental to double the monthly profit of a long-term rental property. We were making around $900 per month with long-term tenants. Once we converted to short term, we've had months more than $3,000 in income (per property).

2. **Less wear and tear on the property:** Usually, short-term guests bring a suitcase and a few carry-on bags. Guests aren't moving in furniture or painting rooms. Plus, short term rental guests are usually in the area to sightsee and splurge at restaurants. Unless there is inclement weather, they are rarely there.

3. **Calendar flexibility:** It is very simple to block off dates that

your property is available. If you have friends or family wanting to stay at your property, simply block off those dates and use the space for your loved ones.

4. **Many tax write offs:** Furniture, utilities, cleaning fees, cable/internet, streaming services all become tax write offs. This helps reduce your taxable income with Uncle Sam.

SHORT TERM RENTAL CONS

1. **Less passive:** Being a short-term rental landlord puts you in the hospitality business. If you leave home without your phone or don't have internet access, you risk losing business. Being on platforms like Airbnb and VRBO requires you to be ready to handle guest questions and problems at any hour.

2. **Expensive to launch:** What will separate your property from the hotel down the road? Upgrades, renovations, and having a comfy and fun vibe goes a long way in making a good impression. It isn't unusual for an STR host to spend $20,000 on home furnishings, decor and upgrading the kitchen or bathrooms.

3. **More work:** This isn't "mailbox money." You must constantly look at the supply and demand of the local prices to make your property competitive. This requires basic research and switching up prices on the rental property calendar. Dave spends around an hour each week per property.

4. **Becoming too reliant on others:** Like any investment, be cautious of putting all of your eggs in one basket. Don't rely strictly on platforms like Airbnb and VRBO to find guests, create your own website for guests to book directly with you.

LONG-TERM RENTALS (LTR'S)

Long-term rentals are generally considered to be a lease of six months and beyond. A long-term rental might require less work, but could render a smaller, albeit potentially steadier, return on your investment. If you are investing in an area that will not attract the short-term rental crowds, the long-term rental business might be for you. With one tenant leasing for a year, your long-term property will not be cleaned or checked as often as a short-term rental will be, meaning stronger wear and tear. A portion of your profit will need to be placed in a sinking fund to take care of potential damage between tenants.

LONG TERM RENTAL PROS

1. **Way more passive than STR's:** Besides collecting rent and occasionally driving by to check on the property, long term tenants are basically on autopilot.

2. **More stable and steady:** A roof over your head is one of the core human needs. With less and less Americans interested in buying, they will need a long-term solution and your property could be their solution. We once had the same renter for five consecutive years and are still friends to this day.

3. **Less upfront costs:** Most long-term rentals are not fully furnished, and you don't have to worry about star ratings from guests nor do you need the latest decor or fancy appliances.

LONG TERM RENTAL CONS

1. **Less income:** In the right location, an STR could make 2x or 3x the monthly rent.

2. **More wear and tear on property:** Tenants moving big furniture in and out, hanging pictures and the wear and tear of being at the property eight+ hours a day will take a toll on walls, appliances, and carpets.

3. **Heavy workload when transitioning from one tenant to the next:** In my experience, it usually takes around $2,000 and a few weeks to get a property "right" after a year of a long-term guest staying. Paint, carpets cleaned, patching holes, etc. can delay the move in date for the next tenant.

4. **Less tax write-offs:** For long term guests, you likely aren't paying utility bills, cleaners, or other housing basics. That is up to the tenant. You can write off your taxes, insurance, and mortgage interest.

CHECKLIST FOR GETTING INTO
THE RENTAL REAL ESTATE GAME

1. Location, location, location!

2. Financing. If you plan to finance a short-term rental, you will need to consider the risk. The FIT Position is to never put yourself in a position to be dependent upon the rent to make the mortgage. We never advocate for speculation or gambling. You might be speculating that you can make enough off the short-term rental business to pay a second mortgage but that is a gamble and will over-leverage you as a middle-income earner. Rental property usually requires a minimum of 20% down.

3. Consider maintenance, yard work, house cleaning and turnover between guests. Calculate how much time you have for these things and whether you will need to hire people to help you.

4. Consider the price point. How much can you reasonably charge in your area to stay busy, and how much do you need to turn a profit?

5. Marketing strategies. How will you advertise your short-term rental to make sure that you are keeping a steady flow of customers and what can you do to make sure that your guests have a great stay ensuring a five-star review?

6. Check with your local government. Some municipalities will not allow short term rentals.

7. Will you self-manage or hire a property manager? Property management will take a chunk of your profit.

HOUSE FLIPPING

Flipping homes could be a great option, especially if you have a strong background in home building and repair. Flipping homes is usually more speculative than buying long and short-term rental real estate. In many cases, house flipping isn't readily available. Some homes are in such need of repair that the bank won't let you borrow money for the purchase. I've never "flipped" a home, but I know many people who have. Based on their experience, consider having multiple partners or investors. This strategy reduces your profit, but also reduces your risk. Multiple partners can bring forth a different set of skills to help with the division of labor.

You never know if a project will cost more than you expected, or if it will render the profit that you were hoping for. Many of these purchases are "sight unseen" and you never get a chance to get inside the property before your offer is accepted. The speculative nature of house flipping isn't for everyone.

IS REAL ESTATE INVESTING REALISTIC?

One way to get around a large 20% down payment is to purchase a property as your primary residence. This will cost you, potentially, only 3.5% or less on a down payment. After you live in the home for a period, you can buy another home to live in as your primary residence while renting the old property out.

When I met my wife at 25 years old, she already owned a small townhome. At that time, I feared real estate. She convinced me to buy a townhouse rather than continuing to make my landlord wealthy. Once married, my wife moved into my townhouse, and we decided to rent out her old residence. After a year of living in my townhome together, we decided to build a small 1600 square foot patio home. When the new construction project was complete, we repeated the process of what we did with her property and rented out my townhome.

In three years, I went from being a renter who was afraid to buy a home to having three properties, two that were rentals, and one that was our primary residence. The move has paid dividends as our real estate portfolio is now worth a million dollars. Because the initial purchases were primary homes at the time, we were able to do this without ever having to put down 20%. The market was favorable during this time, but our combined adjusted gross income was below $100,000. We went from zero to three homes very quickly, even on a middle-income salary.

PLAN FOR THE UNEXPECTED

Tenants can be unpredictable and things in your home will

break or need fixed. Be sure to have a sinking fund to go toward repairs, unpaid rent, or other unexpected events. If your mortgage is $900 and the rent you collect is $1,200, that doesn't mean you have an extra $300 per month to go out to eat. You will need to put the majority of that "cash flow" away for a rainy day. We always have a $5,000 emergency savings account for each rental property we own.

CHAPTER TWELVE ACTION STEPS

1. Know yourself. Rental real estate isn't for everyone. Are you built for it? If so, do you want more hands on (short term) or more passive (long term) rentals?

2. Assess your real estate situation. What is the most feasible way to get in the real estate game? Sell your house? Add a roommate? Fix up the basement? Add an ADU?

3. If you own, have a real state agent price your home to assess its worth. Next, look at how much you owe. Determine how much money you'd make if the home was sold. Could the earnings be enough to buy a primary AND rental?

4. Identify properties in your area and see if they meet the 1% rule. Practice by looking up properties online and run the numbers.

5. Start a sinking fund for a rental real estate down payment.

6. Determine what type of rental market is in your area. Is there more of a need for short term rentals or long term?

7. If you are nervous about doing this alone, find a team of friends/family who might want to go on this journey with you

8. Plan for the unexpected. Have emergency reserves to protect yourself.

IMPERATIVE #3
BE A LIFELONG LEARNER

"For us is the life of action, of strenuous performance of duty; let us live in the harness, striving mightily; let us run the risk of wearing out rather than rusting out."
~Theodore Roosevelt

Being frugal will get you a healthy gap number, being fearless will help you to add to that gap number and parlay it into wealth, but being a lifelong learner will give you the ability to stay the course and grow as time goes on.

We have had the opportunity to meet many teachers and middle-income earners over the past two years that are winning with money. They have all been frugal, fearless, and lifelong learners. They all read books, or listen to podcasts, and they are open to new ideas and new ways of doing things. We have found that many of our listeners are not just looking to learn new things. They listen each week to gain encouragement and inspiration to stay the course.

Being a lifelong learner is more than just a person that reads and listens to podcasts. Lifelong learners are driven by action. They want to get involved. They want to make an impact. Lifelong learners strive for growth. There is a connection between learning and action. Theodore Roosevelt read one to three books a day. He had an insatiable passion for learning. He also had an insatiable passion for action.

Lifelong learners are motivated by the idea of doing something positive. They get excited about something and then they pursue it passionately. They never quit when faced with unexpected challenges. In fact, they live for the challenge. Lifelong learners are also drawn to one another. They often meet on the way to doing some good for the world, or on the path to advancing a worthy cause. Every lifelong learner out there is not winning with money, but everyone out there that is winning with money is a lifelong learner.

Ramsey Solutions conducted the largest survey of millionaires ever done and when the data was in, teachers were the third most represented profession on the list. I was blown away when I first read this. I questioned it. How could that be true? Teachers do not make much money. How could a teacher become a net-worth millionaire?

Teachers are lifelong learners. They are problem solvers. They strive to make an impact and they are excited about what they do. In fact, many teachers are not winning with money because they are so hyper-focused on teaching their students and on other causes in their life that they ignore their own finances. They accept the conventional wisdom that suggests that teachers can't build wealth and they take a vow of poverty, sacrificing themselves for the good of the profession. Teachers that are winning with money have refused to accept conventional wisdom. They set out to prove the masses wrong. They became passionate about solving the economic problem facing teachers and other middle-income earners. It should come as no surprise that they have solved the problem to the tune of net-worth millionaire status. Only the engineering and accounting professions have produced more net-worth millionaires in America.

LIFELONG LEARNERS AND WILD CARDS

Lifelong learners oftentimes put themselves in situations to discover their wildcard. They do not sit on the sidelines. They are rolling up their sleeves and involving themselves with other lifelong learners to advance a cause. They are working for charitable organizations, advocating for issues that they believe in, serving on boards and committees, running for office, or helping a candidate run a campaign... whatever they passionately believe in, they are out doing it. It should come as no surprise that involvement leads to opportunity. Wildcards are a product of the opportunity presented to those that are willing to work.

My first wildcard on this journey to becoming financially independent was *The Financially Independent Teachers Podcast*. I had no idea that Dave's invitation to do this with him would change my life so profoundly. I believed in the cause, and reluctantly accepted his invitation. The work that we have done, and the people that we have met, have changed my life for the better. And, if it had not been for the podcast, I would have never become reacquainted with the woman that I'm going to marry. Lori Ann has become my second wildcard because I'm a better person with her in my life. She is the greatest thing that has ever happened to me on every front. It seems that one wildcard can lead to more. From what I know about the stories of those that we have interviewed, and my own story, lifelong learning leads to action, action leads to wildcards, and wildcards lead to a life never dreamed of.

"I am a great believer in luck, and I find that the harder I work the more of it I have."
~Thomas Jefferson

CHAPTER THIRTEEN
SHIFT HAPPENS

"You cannot be mentally healthy without a routine."
~Jordan Peterson

As we kick off the third imperative, I need to confess to something: I have always hated money. There, I said it. I hate it. I hate that I need it. I hate what I have imagined that it does to people. I hate spending time thinking about it. I have always avoided talking about money like the plague. I love reading about history, politics, certain fields of science, literature, short-stories, economics, philosophy, and topics in Christianity, just to name a few. But personal finances? That is a subject that I always turned my nose up at. I have always spent money on books, but I didn't buy my first personal finance book until I was 43-years old... and desperate.

My disdain for money led me to think as little about it as possible. I put all my bills on auto draft and scheduled them to hit at the beginning of each month. I then spent money and hoped that I had enough to make it until the next paycheck. I rarely did and finished most months out using credit cards. I was busy doing things that I enjoyed doing, so I didn't have time to concern myself with something that I couldn't achieve success with anyway. That was my philosophy for many years. Really stupid.

When it comes to your financial situation, it is a good idea to carve out time daily to check your accounts and your spending against your budget so that you can stay on top of things. As a lifelong learner, you should be constantly evaluating yourself.

Self-reflection is key. Whether we like it or not, the one constant in life is change. As life events happen, we need to continually reassess our financial situation. There are six things that you should be checking on a regular basis.

YOUR BUDGET

Whenever I ask someone specific questions about their budget and they can't give me quick, exact answers, I know that they don't have a budget. Let me tell you, this is almost everyone. I have met very few people that have a budget.

Lori Ann and I have decided that I will take primary responsibility for our budget. She is more than capable, and much smarter than I am, but she would prefer that I do it, and I'm happy to take on that responsibility so that she doesn't have to think about it. She and I will sit down every year to think through the calendar and come up with our annual budget. She and I will also sit down every month for our "monthly budget review." If that is all that we did, we would be doing better than most, but we still wouldn't have a real budget. I will be carving out 15 minutes a day to review all of our accounts and spending against our WRITTEN budget to make sure that we are on track. By planning an annual budget meeting, and doing monthly budget reviews, we will be reducing the number of times that we are taken by surprise by the unexpected. But life still happens. Daily check-ins are necessary to stay on track.

Changes in life can happen quickly, and we must be ready to adjust. As I'm writing this, we have experienced rapid inflation and the increase in prices on everything has created the need for adjustments in our budget. I am spending $200-$300 more each month at the gas pump than I was a year ago. Groceries, sundry items, gas, you name it, are all much more expensive now than they were a short time ago. There are so many things that are common to life that can impact your budget and cause things to change. You might have been executing a budget successfully for years and then find out that you will be welcoming new life into the world. Diapers, formula, wipes, and the cost of daycare will likely be a budget buster. Before you know it, the baby will be off to kindergarten. Time to adjust the budget again.

The first thing that you must keep learning about is your own life and circumstances. Things never stay the same. It isn't fun, but you must stay on top of your budget in order to make sure that an ever-changing world doesn't get you off track. When it comes to investing, we always say "set it and forget." Your budget doesn't work that way. You can't flip the autopilot switch.

YOUR INSURANCE (RISK MANAGEMENT PLAN)

Middle-income earners should have, or at least consider, six insurance policies:

1. **Health Insurance:** as a teacher this is probably part of your benefit package. If you are a teacher in North Carolina, your health insurance, at the time that I'm writing this, is pretty good. Dave and I are both on the North Carolina Blue Cross Blue Shield 70/30 Plan. In the next chapter, you will see from Dave and Stephanie's story what a blessing our health insurance is.

2. **Term-Life Insurance:** this is very important if you are married or have anyone that depends on your income. If you have a mortgage, term-life insurance is also very important. In this book we have avoided prescriptions, so we won't say how much term-life insurance you need, but here are some things to consider: how would you handle losing your spouse? Are you going to be ready to go back to work after the funeral? Can you afford your mortgage payment on one salary? If you have children, what will they need if they lose you or your spouse sooner than expected? Do you need a term-life policy for your child? If you lost a child, would you be ready to go back to work after the funeral? These are tough topics, and no one enjoys talking about them. Marriages often end after the death of a child. People can easily fall apart when they lose a spouse. Term-life insurance is not just about the funeral. It is about the life that goes on after the loss of a loved one and being realistic about what you will need.

3. **Disability Insurance:** what happens if you get injured and can't come to work? Could you survive without a check for a year? Dave carried disability insurance for most of his young career. After accumulating a year of sick leave, he decided to drop the policy and save the $44 per month.

4. **Car Insurance:** if you drive, you need to have liability. If you don't have a car note, you can drop the collision, but should you? Only if you can afford to replace the car or have work done on it should you have an accident that is your fault.

5. **Renters Insurance or Home Insurance:** if you are renting, renters' insurance is a no-brainer. It is cheap and valuable should something happen. If you are renting and something happens to the home you are renting, your landlord's insurance will not cover your belongings. If you have a mortgage, you have to have home insurance. Even after the mortgage is paid off, you will still need home insurance. Dropping it is a risk that few middle-income earners can afford.

There are basically two types of people when it comes to insurance: (A) those that like to have all their insurance needs covered by the same company and they have them all with the same agent, and (B) those that constantly shop around for the best deals.

All my insurance policies are parked in one place. I love the company, I have one agent that handles all my insurance needs, and I can call or text him anytime and know that he will respond in a reasonable amount of time. I love that. I could probably find cheaper rates elsewhere, but I value the relationship that I have with my agent and the company that I am with. There is nothing wrong with shopping around for the best rates on each policy that you don't have through your employer. It involves a little more work, but it is a way to save money.

Everyone needs to think about their situation and decide if they need more insurance or possibly less insurance. As the world turns, and your situation changes, so might your insurance needs. Your risk management plan doesn't require the same level of attention as your budget, but it does require you to be aware of what you are paying for and what your needs are.

YOUR CREDIT SCORE

The higher your credit score, the better. A perfect credit score (FICO score) is 850. You don't need an 850 to be considered someone who has "good credit." 740+ is a very good place to be. So many things affect your credit score. In general, paying your bills on time, having low utilization (you have access to credit that you aren't using), accounts that are old, and an overall history of being responsible with credit will give you a good credit score. I check my credit score every three months. I get a report through my Mint account (mentioned in Imperative #1), and I get a report from The State Employees Credit Union where I have my checking account. As I was becoming debt free (and achieved debt free status) my credit score was consistently on the rise. In recent months my score has taken a hit because I have had to take on some debt again. Paying that debt off is a primary goal of mine. I might be in the market for a new home soon and I want my credit score to be as good as it can be for that reason. A quality credit score can secure lower interest rates on loans, and credit cards.

YOUR BILLS AND EXPENSES

During the 15-minutes that I will be carving out every day to check our budget, I will also be opening every piece of mail that arrives at the house. We live in a world that is becoming increasingly less professional. Mistakes can be made under the best of circumstances, and we aren't living under the best of circumstances. It is a good idea to stay on top of every bill to make sure that you aren't being overcharged for anything. I stay on top of all we are being charged for so that I can discover mistakes, but also so that I can identify changes in how much we are being charged, and the services that we are getting. I dropped cable a long time ago because rates kept climbing. I have canceled subscriptions for the same reason.

Have you ever thrown a check away because you thought it was junk mail? I have. Again, open all mail. I have a place in the house with a desk, computer, trashcan, and a paper shredder. That is where I sit and open mail and check my accounts.

Bills and expenses change all the time, and you should be ready to change with them.

YOUR BENEFITS PACKAGE

When we get hired, there is usually a meeting with HR to discuss your benefits. You get a large folder with tons of paperwork that you likely never read. We've discovered many teachers don't understand their benefits. Ask one question about any part of your teacher benefits in a state-specific Facebook group and you'll get 25 different answers. The confusion around our North Carolina teacher benefits prompted Dave to create a North Carolina Benefits Workshop for teachers that he offers from time to time. To date, almost 1,000 NC educators have taken part. **Check the Financially Independent Teachers website to see if the next workshop fits your schedule.**

Many of the benefits available to you are based on your hiring date. For example, North Carolina teachers hired BEFORE January 1, 2021, will have access to North Carolina health benefits in retirement. Unfortunately, new teachers in our state no longer qualify for this benefit. Become an expert in your benefits and more specifically, understand your unique benefits based on your hire date.

If you don't feel confident in understanding your benefits, this is completely normal. Dave spent countless hours understanding his sick leave, pension, and retirement benefits. In 2019, Dave's family was rocked to the core when his wife was diagnosed with breast cancer. Even though he thought he had a solid foundation of knowledge of his benefits package, he quickly discovered he knew almost nothing about the details of his state health plan. The news of a serious medical condition is already stressful enough. If you don't understand your benefits and deductibles, it only adds more tension and anxiety. At the time of diagnosis, Dave was signed up with the NC 70/30 plan. In his mind, he thought that out of the $1,000,000 of upcoming medical debt, he would be responsible for $300,000 or 30%. The state would cover the other 70%. Dave's "out of pocket max" or the most he would be responsible for in a calendar year was $6,000. In the end, Dave's insurance covered $994,000 of the one million dollars of medical bills. Protect your family by having enough money in emergency savings to cover your out-of-pocket max in the case of a medical situation.

RULE CHANGES

When it comes to your investments, set it and forget it, but be aware of changes in how much you can set your allocations for. When we first started recording our podcast, for example, the maximum amount that you could invest per year in an IRA if you were under age 50 was $6,000. Now it is $6,500 (2023). If you were maxing out your IRA, and you can throw that extra $500 in there, you would probably want to do that. Also, once you've made your 50th trip around the sun, you qualify to add more into your tax shelters.

ROUTINES FOR THE WIN

As mentioned, having routines is so important if you are going to stay on top of things. For some, this comes naturally. For people like me, it doesn't. I must impose order on my life or chaos ensues. With the following action steps in mind, I have built a set of routines for myself to make sure that I can respond to the ever-changing world around me. Lifelong learners are always working to stay updated on their situation to make sure that their actions are working in concert with reality. This takes work, but isn't anything that is worth having?

CHAPTER THIRTEEN ACTION STEPS

1. Carve out 15-minutes a day to review your budget against your daily spending.

2. During your 15-minutes a day open all the mail that comes your way and dispose of what isn't needed. Have a routine for steps one and two.

3. Review your insurance needs and what you are paying for insurance on a regular basis. Your risk management plan is important and can't be completely forgotten about.

4. Keep track of your credit score and how your habits are affecting it. Make corrections in your day-to-day life that will positively impact your credit score.

5. Be sure to review your benefits package from time to time to make sure that you understand it and be aware of any changes that are occurring. Annual Open Enrollment periods are a good time to do this.

6. If you are a North Carolina teacher, take the FIT NC Teacher's Benefits Training so that you can better understand your benefits package better.

7. Check your investment allocations to make sure that you are matching the increases the government might be making to how much you can invest in the tax shelters that you are utilizing.

CHAPTER FOURTEEN
REVERSE ENGINEERING YOUR CAREER

"Begin with the end in mind."
~Stephen Covey

Dave told me a story once that has stuck with me. He was just beginning his second year as a classroom teacher. He was in his early 20s. The central office in Onslow County, where he has worked for his entire career, held a meeting for anyone that wanted to learn more about the North Carolina retirement plan for teachers. Approximately 20 people showed up to the meeting. All 20 were obviously aging teachers approaching retirement... and Dave. They asked him, "why would a young guy like you be thinking about retirement?" Dave said, "because I don't want to wait until the end of my career to start figuring this stuff out. I want to know in advance so that I can prepare for it."

Dave has been a lifelong learner from day one. That meeting put him on the path that he is currently traveling on. He learned many things in that meeting that prompted him to keep learning. Most people avoid meetings like the plague. Especially meetings on subjects that are 25-30 years out. Dave intuitively knew something that many of his colleagues didn't. Dave knew that he needed to reverse engineer his career or mistakes would be made. He is now an expert on the North Carolina benefits package and that, along with all the other things that he has been inspired to learn on his path towards retirement, has enabled him to be able to retire comfortably at age 50.

Your budget should begin with the end in mind. To build your budget around your saving and investing goals, you should try to answer these three questions: **How old do you want to be when you retire? What will be your projected expenses in retirement? What kind of lifestyle would you like to lead in retirement?** Once you answer these questions, you can work backwards and figure out what you need to do to get where you want to go. You will have to make constant adjustments. Again, you won't be able to "set it, and forget it." There is no autopilot switch. Your success will be dependent on your willingness to consistently reevaluate your situation and adjust. In addition, learning new things, and putting new lessons into action will change the trajectory of your path. The lifelong learner will set out with a destination in mind but will usually end up in a far better place than originally dreamed.

REVERSE ENGINEERING

You always want to begin with the end in mind. Create a budget that is built around saving and investment goals. These goals are informed by the retirement age expected and what will be needed to supplement pensions and social security to live your desired lifestyle in retirement. Understanding your pension and how much money you can expect to draw during your retirement years will reveal what else might be needed in the way of investments. Each state has a different pension plan, and in some states, teachers are also paying into social security. If you desire to retire at the age of 50, for example, it will be necessary to discover what your pension payout will be per month if you retire at that age and how much money you expect to need to live the lifestyle that you desire in retirement. This information will reveal how much additional income you will need to supplement your pension. This is what is meant by *reverse engineering* your career.

YOUR HOUSE

By retirement, you should strive to have your primary residence paid off. There are many all over America that have secured 30-year mortgages in their 40s and 50s. They could have paid off their home in their 50s and been able to use their last decade of work to save and invest at a rate that would have allowed them to be very comfortable in retirement. Instead, they will be paying their mortgage into their 70s and 80s and will likely have to work during their retirement years because they just had to have that dream house. I wonder how great those granite counter tops look on the way out the door at age 72 to go work a job not cared for?

Dave and I hear people with two or more kids complain all the time about the size of their homes. They imagine that they NEED a larger home. Here is a truth bomb that American families need to hear: love grows best in small homes. In the 1950s, the average American home was around 1,000 square feet. Today, the average US home is over 2,200 square feet. Every kid does not need their own room, and you do not need all the space that you think you need to entertain. People always imagine that they will entertain often, and so they buy a large house with that in mind, and they are lucky to host four larger gatherings a year. Probably not a good investment.

The FIT Position on housing is that a simple home that is paid for is far better than a "dream home" that you are paying for long into retirement. Paying off your primary residence before you retire is a major step towards financial independence. A mortgage payment is usually the largest check that you write each month.

DEBT FREE LIFE

By the time you are ready to retire, you should have been executing a budget for many years that has afforded you a debt-free lifestyle, or a mostly debt-free lifestyle. To do this, you will need to live a frugal lifestyle. You will need to drive reasonably inexpensive cars. Yes, you want a reliable car. No, you do not need to go into serious debt to secure one. That is an excuse for spending too much money. If you are concerned about being stranded on the highway, invest in AAA. Or look at your car insurance policy. Car insurance policies often come with roadside assistance.

Take reasonably priced vacations. You can camp out in a state park and make memories and enjoy all that a state park has to offer. No lines. No crowds. And spend a fraction of the cost of going to see the famous mouse... and a fraction of the headache. State parks are just one example of an easy vacation that will not require a small fortune. There are many other examples.

The point is that we must start questioning conventional wisdom. Conventional wisdom is what the masses follow, and the masses are broke and in debt.

THE FRUIT OF YOUR SACRIFICE AND LABOR

Throughout the course of your working years, you should have sacrificed "things and stuff" but not joy. You drove inexpensive cars, lived in a simple home, took less expensive vacations, ate cheap, nutritious meals at home, and did not spend your money on income-sucking toys. And yet, your photo albums are somehow still full. You valued the people in your lives, not the stuff you bought or the destinations that you traveled to. This shift in mindset leads to a fuller and richer life. Is there even a reasonable argument in favor of "stuff" over relationships? This is what has become glaringly obvious after more than 100 hours of published podcast content: that is, that middle-income earners that are winning with money care more about the right things and less about the things that don't matter in the long run.

As a middle-income earner, you will need to sacrifice some of the "stuff" to achieve financial independence and security. Teachers are better in the classroom when they are not in debt. Debt, and financial woes, are a heavy burden and make life difficult. It is hard to be the parent that you want to be under the stress of debt. It is difficult to be the spouse that you want to be or anything else when debt hangs over you like the rain cloud that followed Charlie Brown. When you are allocating 20% or more of your income to savings and investing goals, you are purchasing freedom, peace of mind, and stability. The fruit of your sacrifice and labor is great mental health, which is priceless.

REASONABLE SAVINGS AND INVESTING GOALS

How much you need to save and invest depends upon when you start saving and investing, how much you net monthly, and when you want to retire. Most career teachers have a pension to look forward to, and many will have paid into social security as well. The circumstances surrounding your current situation will dictate, to some degree, what is possible for you in terms of retirement.

THE 4% RULE

This rule has become famous. Based on historical returns in the market, if you withdraw 4% of the money that you have invested every year, it is almost a sure thing that your money will never dwindle, and that it will in fact continue to grow. If you only withdraw 3%, that "almost" becomes close to a guarantee.

If Dave has $200,000 in his Roth IRA by the time he retires at age 62, according to the 4% rule he can withdraw $8,000 (4% of 200k) at the beginning of each year to supplement his pension and social security. What will happen to his investment total in that next year? It will, very likely, grow back to $200,000. It is also very possible that by the next year he might have a total of more than $200,000. Of course, there will be some years sprinkled in that will see his investments take a loss.

If you retire from a career that does not offer a pension, your investments become so much more important. Your 4% will not be icing on the cake. You will have to live off 4% of your investments every year. Your social security check will supplement your investments but will not likely be enough for you to live on. If you have $1,000,000 invested by the time you retire, you will be able to withdraw $40,000 a year to live on. Do you want $80,000 per year to live on? Then you need $2,000,000 invested.

If you are reading this book, and you are in your 40s or 50s, and you have no pension coming, and no investments to speak of, you are certainly in a tough spot. You need to go create an account with www.ssa.gov and see what you can expect your social security check to look like. For you to retire at all, you will need to get your bills and expenses under that number. In addition, you need to find a way to invest a great deal of money over the next 10-20 years while also making sure that you are debt free. Dave and I started this podcast, and are writing this book, in part, to make sure that fewer people are staring down this scenario.

THE 25X RULE

How will you know if you are ready to retire? Ultimately, financial independence isn't an age, it is a number, and you can't get there by luck. The earlier you start planning for the end of your career, the easier this process will be. The Rule of 25 (25x) states that individuals are recommended to have 25x their annual spending saved before retirement. First, you will need to know how much you ACTUALLY spend each year (Imperative #1). Let's say you would like to have $40,000 per year in retirement. That means you will need to have $1,000,000 ($40k x 25) in investments before you sail off into the sunset. Circling back to your primary home... having your home paid off before you exit the workforce will pay major dividends. A paid off primary home will greatly reduce the amount of money needed in investments to supplement your annual income. Renting serves its purpose in many seasons of life, but you will never rid yourself of what is likely your largest monthly expenditure when renting.

Below, you will see a comparison between two individuals; one carries a mortgage into retirement and the other does not.

Janice	Jessica
Total Monthly Spending = $4,000	Total Monthly Spending = $2,500
Total Monthly Mortgage = $1,500	Total Monthly Mortgage = $0
Total Annual Spending = $48,000	Total Annual Spending = $30,000
Investments For 25x Rule = $1,200,000	Investments For 25x Rule = $750,000

As you can see, having your home paid off BEFORE reaching retirement age lowers the amount needed, when following the 25x

Rule. Jessica's paid off mortgage reduced her investment need by $450,000.

THE FIT 10X PENSION RULE

If you are a middle-income earner working in the private sector (without a pension), the 25x Rule can be intimidating. On the other hand, teachers with a pension have access to a 25x cheat code. Many teachers are unaware of how valuable their pension is. If you have access to a pension, we've changed the 25x rule to the 10x rule. Let's assume you want your projected annual spending in retirement to be $60,000 per year. Following the advice of the 25x Rule, you would need $1,500,000 ($60,000 x 25) in investments to comfortably retire. For many, that number would seem daunting. Remember, the 25x Rule does not account for a pension.

The FIT 10x Rule makes the above situation less daunting. Teachers, your pension is a financial superpower. According to the FIT 10x Rule, a teacher wanting a lifestyle of around $60,000 per year (with a pension) would only need $600,000 ($60,000 x 10) saved in investment accounts. If Dave teaches 30 years in North Carolina, his projected pension will be approximately $36,000 per year. With a $36,000 a year pension and $600,000 of investments, Dave and Stephanie would actually have $60,000 a year to spend. This is following the guidelines of the 4% rule that was mentioned above and doesn't include any social security earnings at 62+. Once you add in social security, they will have even more monthly income.

NC Teacher Pension = $36,000 Per Year

4% of $600,000 Invested = $24,000 Per Year

NC Pension + 4% Rule ($600,000) = $60,000 Per Year

PENSION

If you have a pension, it is imperative to reverse engineer and understand the age in which you have access and how much the monthly payout will be. If teaching two more years means you'll make an extra $600 per month for the rest of your life, it might be worth it. If you find out it only makes a $150 per month difference, maybe you ride off into the sunset early? Dave will have access to his pension starting at 50 years of age. At 50, Dave's NC pension will likely be $3,000 per month, after taxes. This ends up being a net of $36,000 per year. On the flip side, if Dave teaches until he is 55, he will net closer to $41,000 per year in retirement. Each state is different, but the current North Carolina pension formula is your highest four year (consecutive) gross salary average x 0.182 x years of service. In the state of North Carolina, coaching, annual leave payout and other school supplements will count toward your highest four-year average. If in North Carolina, create an account at https://orbit.myncretirement.com/ to see where you stand with your numbers.

SOCIAL SECURITY

If you have paid into social security, create an account at www. ssa.gov to see what your projected monthly social security check will look like. Social Security is based on your lifetime earnings, indexed to average the highest 35 earning years of your working career. Age 62 is the magic number to access social security. Depending on your unique situation, you might be able to wait until your full retirement age (FRA) to touch your social security. Each year you wait (beyond 62), your social security benefit increases by approximately 8% per year. As North Carolina educators, we will be eligible to collect social security and the NC pension. Taking social security early at 62 provides the smallest monthly benefit. Drawing early on your social security will limit how much you can earn per year (without paying some money back to the government). If you wait until your FRA, you can make as much money as you want in a year. Some want to get their hard-earned money back as soon as they can, others prefer to wait.

Based on Dave's current numbers, he is expecting to make $1,600 per month in social security at age 62 and $3,000 per month at age 50 from his North Carolina pension. This means Dave will have a combined (gross) annual income of approximately

$55,200 at age 62. If Dave waits to collect social security until age 67 (FRA), his social security check increases to $2,400 per month. Dave might start collecting at 62, five years earlier than his FRA age of 67. Consider this: a married NC teacher couple with 30 years of service in the state + social security can expect an annual retirement income of nearly $100,000 at age 62... that is the equivalent of having 2.76 million dollars invested, based on the 4% rule. As financial coaches, we have worked with many NC teachers with their pension and social security projections. Based on our experiences, we have created a case study to show what "could be" in the case of a married NC teacher couple who will have a pension + social security.

Case Study: Married NC Teacher Couple
30 Years of Service, Taking Social Security at 62

NC Teacher #1	NC Teacher #2
NC Retirement Pension = $3,000	NC Retirement Pension = $3,000
Social Security Benefits @ 62 = $1,600	Social Security Benefits @ 62 = $1,600
Total Monthly Income @ 62 = $4,600	Total Monthly Income @ 62 = $4,600
Combined Total Monthly Income @ 62 = $9,200 **Combined Total Annual Income @ 62 = $110,400**	

Taking SS early at 62 will limit the amount of money you can "earn" if you are wanting to continue to work as you collect early SS. Your pension benefits do not count as "income." Delaying SS to full retirement age will allow you to continue to earn as much as you want in your 60s and have a larger SS paycheck in the future.

Case Study: Married NC Teacher Couple
30 Years of Service, Taking Social Security at 67

NC Teacher #1	NC Teacher #2
NC Retirement Pension = $3,000	NC Retirement Pension = $3,000
Social Security Benefits @67 = $2,400	Social Security Benefits @67 = $2,400
Total Monthly Income @ 67 = $5,400	Total Monthly Income @ 67 = $5,400
Combined Total Monthly Income @ 67 = $10,800 **Combined Total Annual Income @ 67 = $129,600**	

If you are a teacher with a pension AND social security with NO investments, there is HOPE! Even if this teacher couple NEVER invested a dime for their future selves, they will still have a respectable quality of life that is better than most. Don't rely on this alone, it is never too late to open a Roth IRA if you still have "earned" income. If you are someone concerned about generational social mobility, your pension and SS alone won't do much to help pass wealth on to your children and grandchildren. Imagine if this couple had investments to go along with all the above?

It is very possible for a retired teacher couple to have $130,000-$150,000 a year to spend in retirement.

GENERATIONAL SOCIAL MOBILITY

As we approach the final seasons of our lives, we inevitably begin to think about what we will leave behind for our children, grandchildren, and possibly the other children in our families. There is no reason why your family cannot be in the wealthiest 5%, or greater, in three generations or less. Generational social mobility is something to consider. If you can live off your pension, social security, and 4% or less of your investments, you will be leaving behind enough money to give the next generation in your family a wonderful head start.

What happens to your Roth IRA when you die? You can leave it behind to someone and then they can let it continue to grow for 10 years before they must withdraw the funds. Here is the exciting part: your money in the stock market, in a good index fund, will roughly double every eight to ten years (Rule of 72). The Rule of 72 is a formula that calculates how long it will take for an investment to double in value, based on its rate of return.

CHAPTER FOURTEEN ACTION STEPS

1. Create an account at www.ssa.gov and see your projected social security numbers. Use these numbers to help assist your future financial plan.

2. Run your pension numbers. If you are a North Carolina teacher, create an account at orbit.myncretirement.com.

3. Identify the age at which you would like to retire.

4. Identify how much money you will need to live the lifestyle that you want to live in retirement.

5. Continue to develop the habit of frugality right where you are.

6. Keep executing a good budget.

7. Make plans to pay off a primary residence before retirement. The earlier, the better!

8. Set up your investments with the 4% rule in mind, taking into consideration what your retirement needs will be and when you want to retire.

CHAPTER FIFTEEN
INVEST IN YOURSELF

"The best investment you can make, is an investment in
yourself... The more you learn, the more you'll earn."
~**Warren Buffett**

By reading this book, you have invested in yourself. The greatest
wealth-building tool that you have is your brain and your physical capabilities. Maxing out the potential of both is paramount.
As teachers, one of our top priorities should be to motivate our
students to become lifelong learners. Lifelong learners win with
money, and they win in everything else that they do.

When you invest in yourself, you can expect a return. In fact,
you can expect interest on your return to compound over time.
Those that invest in themselves in an intentional way can stay the
course and win with money, and anything else that they endeavor
to do.

Here are a few ways that you can actively, and intentionally,
invest in yourself:

READ BOOKS

When we read, we learn empathy as we step into the minds
of countless characters in stories, we learn new skills, we absorb
language that will empower us to become better communicators,
we receive encouragement from the testimony of others, we gain
confidence and are inspired by what we learn is possible, and
we become more aware of who we are and what we value in the

process. Read fiction and non-fiction. Read as often as you can.

There are also books on audio. If you struggle with reading, this could be a great alternative. You can pull up a book on audio and listen to it while you are driving or just accomplishing basic tasks around your home or office.

LISTEN TO PODCASTS

Listening to good podcasts on various subjects will have a similar effect that reading has. For those that struggle to find the time or motivation to read, listening to podcasts can be a reasonable replacement. They are certainly a wonderful supplement to whatever number of books that you read. On the *Financially Independent Teachers Podcast* you will often hear the stories of others, and like reading a biography or autobiography, you can learn in a few minutes what it took someone else years to learn. You should always try to learn from your own mistakes, but it is far better (and less painful) to learn from the mistakes of others.

DEVELOP THE HABIT OF WRITING

We read and listen to podcasts to learn things about the world. We write to learn things about ourselves. Journaling is a wonderful thing to do, although journaling every day about just yourself is probably counter-productive. Writing is thinking. "If you cannot write well, you cannot think well." (George Orwell) Most do not write on a regular basis which would explain why the masses make poor decisions and why conventional wisdom is usually foolish.

A wonderful habit to get into, especially if you are new to investing in yourself, would be to pick a devotional of some kind, or a book that you are interested in, and then write about what you read each day. You can read for as little as 10-15 minutes a day, write a reaction in 10-15 minutes, and in that 20-30 minutes per day you will have invested enough to see unbelievable gains over time. This is very similar to the magic of compound interest in the stock market. The impact that this habit will have on your life is difficult to measure. Your future self will thank you for implementing the routine of reading and writing into your daily life.

YOU ARE THE AVERAGE OF THE FIVE

In the words of Jim Rohn, "You are the average of the five people you spend the most time with." Choose your inner circle wisely. Your inner circle should be composed of good people that are encouraging, positive, and loyal. They should be lifelong learners, and the kind of people that believe in building wealth and giving generously. Obviously, there are many more positive traits, but you get the idea.

When Dave invited me to co-host the *Financially Independent Teachers Podcast*, I had no idea that I was adding such a positive influence into my inner circle. As a result of co-hosting this podcast, I have spent a substantial number of hours with Dave. I had never spent so much time around someone that was a net-worth millionaire that passionately believed that teachers could win with money. The influence that Dave has had in this area of my life has been profound. Simply having a more positive outlook on my own financial journey has made a world of difference. My mental health and outlook on life have improved immensely by adding Dave into my inner circle.

Surround yourself with the right people. Do this by making sure that you are the kind of person that you are looking for. The question is not, "How do I find the right kind of people to surround myself with?" The question is, "How do I become the kind of person that a hardworking, positive, encouraging, and loyal person would want to spend time with? How do I become the kind of person that good people would want around them?" Become that person! Run the right race and the right inner circle of people will find you.

I tell single people to stay away from dating websites. Simply run your race. Become a lifelong learner. Grow. Get action. In the process, look to your left and right. Eventually the man or woman of your dreams will be there. That is exactly what happened to me. I wasn't going to find the woman of my dreams while sitting on the sidelines. I found her while advancing a cause that I believed in.

BE PROACTIVE IN SEARCHING FOR WAYS TO IMPROVE

Warren Buffet, one of the wealthiest people to have ever lived, knew that public speaking was something that he struggled with, and he knew that he needed to work on that. He found a class on public speaking, and he took it. Years later the certificate from that class hangs in his office. He talks about this class as being a great investment that he made in himself, and he has continued to reap the benefits from it. Lifelong learners always look for ways to improve themselves.

YOUR PHYSICAL HEALTH

This is not a health and fitness book, although achieving physical well-being and financial well-being are astonishingly similar. This is an important component of investing in yourself.

I am suggesting to you that you only get one mind and one body. They must last you a lifetime. Take care of them."
~Warren Buffett

There is so much wisdom in this. Buffett said this while talking to a group of young people. We cannot afford bad eating and exercise habits. As it turns out, good eating habits will fit right into your budget goals because, contrary to conventional wisdom, it is cheaper to eat healthy. I can buy a weeks' worth of eggs and pinto beans for the cost of two McDonald's combo meals and the difference in nutritional value is not even on the same planet. Eat healthy food for the health of your budget and body.

In addition, exercise every day in some way. You do not have to train for a marathon or a strong man competition. Just get moving. If you eat right and exercise you will potentially add many years to your life and you will have more energy. More energy and more years led to being more productive. Your physical health is a necessary component in your pursuit of Financial Independence.

There are certainly other health habits that you can adopt that would have a positive impact on your well-being, and other habits that you should break if you have them. The bottom line is, take care of your body.

WHAT DO LIFELONG LEARNERS DO?

After interviewing many teachers that are successful with money we have discovered that most don't listen to podcasts or read books so that they can learn a ton of new information. They continue to listen and read because they know that constant exposure keeps their behavior consistent with what is needed in order to win with money. As a result, they have the following outcomes in common.

THEY GET ACTION

We know that most of personal finance success is not based on knowledge, but behavior. Lifelong learners enjoy the process of learning, and they are truly motivated to put lessons learned into action. Theodore Roosevelt was known for taking action and for his adventurous spirit:

"Get action. Do things; be sane; don't fritter away your time; create, act, take a place wherever you are and be somebody; get action."
~Theodore Roosevelt

Roosevelt acted upon the lessons that he learned. This is a hallmark of the lifelong learner. Teachers are passionate about their classrooms, but we have found that many teachers that are winning with money are passionate about something outside of the classroom. At the very least, they are passionate about building wealth and helping others to do the same.

THEY ARE PASSIONATE GOAL SETTERS

Lifelong learners set goals and pursue them passionately. As educators, we know the benefits of setting goals, writing them down, and pursuing them. We try to get our students to do this, and our efforts are often met with resistance. For so many people setting goals and knowing how to accomplish them is not intuitive. For the lifelong learner, it seems to come naturally. Lifelong learners tend to set goals in all areas of life.

"Without dreams and goals, there is no living,
only merely existing, and that is not why we are here."
~Mark Twain

THEY NATURALLY NETWORK

Lifelong learners are drawn to like-minded people, and they form networks that are beneficial to a cause and on a personal level. We have been amazed at the networking opportunities that have presented themselves by simply starting a podcast for a cause that we believe in. We have had the opportunity to meet some great people that share our desire to see people win with money. We have personally benefited from the "FIT Family." Build a team of good people around you.

THEY SEEK INVOLVEMENT

Lifelong learners cannot sit on the sideline. They must get into the action, and they are often drawn where they can do the most good. They are always on the lookout for opportunities to help others.

THEY ARE POSITIVE

Lifelong learners tend to believe that it is never too late. They anticipate challenges and acknowledge mistakes. The mindset of a lifelong learner is to push for growth and improvement. This results in a positive outlook on life and a belief that with every failure comes hope for victory. If you have ever been around someone like this, it is contagious.

THEY ARE INQUISITIVE AND CURIOUS

Lifelong learners are always asking questions. They look for people that know more than they do, search for books on subjects that they are interested in and are drawn to classes or podcasts that give them insight. They are not afraid to be wrong. Lifelong learners don't care about being right; they just want to get it right.

CHAPTER FIFTEEN ACTION STEPS

1. Develop the habit of reading.

2. Choose a few podcasts to listen to on a regular basis.

3. Develop the habit of writing.

4. Work on bettering yourself which will lead you to the inner circle of people that you need.

5. Take care of your physical health.

6. Get involved in what you are passionate about outside of your classroom/job/career.

7. Write down your goals in all areas of life and work to accomplish them.

8. Build a team of good people around you.

9. Be positive when confronted with challenges.

10. Ask questions, be curious, and do not worry about being wrong.

AFTERWORD
THE FIT POSITION
OUTCOMES

BE FRUGAL

"You say, 'if I had a little more, I should be very satisfied.'
You make a mistake. If you are not content with what
you have, you would not be satisfied if it were doubled."
~Charles Spurgeon

Charles Spurgeon, known as the prince of preachers, preached to thousands of people weekly in London, England in the 1800s. His writing reveals that he was a great observer of human nature. None of his observations could be any truer than this one. More will not make you happy. In fact, with the right mindset, less will.

Living a frugal lifestyle will empower you to execute a budget successfully, spend far less than you make, live debt free, and avoid lifestyle creep. The peace that comes from living within your means, with a healthy gap number to build wealth with, is worth more than all the things and trips that money can buy.

Working the FIT Position into your financial life will not only lead you to a frugal lifestyle but will also lead you into becoming more intentional in spending money on what you value and learning to enjoy life without the expensive bells and whistles. You will discover that a date on the pier eating bacon, lettuce, and tomato sandwiches is every bit as enjoyable as the five-star restaurant experience in Raleigh, North Carolina. Being frugal is imperative if you want to win with money.

BE FEARLESS

"The wild-horse rider is the winner. The wild-horse rider may not be the most talented but will do whatever it takes to get the job done. The wild-horse rider runs toward danger when others are running away and overcomes it. There are not many wild-horse riders out there. They are fearless." ~Jim Sypult

Jim Sypult was my college football coach. He is one of the greatest men that I ever knew. He always told us about the wild-horse rider and how every team needs at least one to win. Coach Sypult was the original wild-horse rider. He was a fearless leader of young men who loved his players and his family passionately and stared down adversity... never backing down an inch.

When you are fearless, you are willing to step out on faith and start that business. You will be able to continue to invest your money in the stock market even when the world is telling you that the market is going to crash. You will have the confidence to STR a home where you will be at the mercy of customers that could give you a one-star review. I've watched Dave and his wife Stephanie make calculated risks with real estate investments, step out on faith, and fearlessly stare down challenges on their way to net-worth millionaire status. Starting our podcast required some guts. It isn't easy to put yourself out there to do something that you believe in. Being fearless is imperative if you want to win with money... or anything else.

It has been said "Scared money don't make no money". As far as I can tell, this is true, but being fearless is easier said than done when you are a middle-income earner.

Once you make up your mind to be fearless, you decide to fail as many times as necessary to be successful. This is the only way that success ever happens. Wild-horse riders get thrown off violently at times, but they never fail to get back on.

BE A LIFELONG LEARNER

"Very early, I knew that the only object in life was to grow. I am suffocated and lost when I have not the bright feeling of progression." ~**Margaret Fuller**

The outcome of being a lifelong learner is a life of growth. Once a lifelong learner believes that they can build wealth and they see the value in doing so, there is no stopping them. We have seen that through the listeners of our podcast. Our listeners are mostly teachers that believe building wealth is possible, and they are on a mission. They are reading books, listening to podcasts, setting goals, joining forces with others that believe that building wealth is possible, and they are asking all the right questions as they take the lessons that they are learning and put them into practice. Being a lifelong learner is imperative to building wealth as a middle-income earner.

CONCLUSION

Dave Fleischer said it best in a post that he made on the *Financially Independent Teachers* Facebook page:

"In the largest study of millionaires ever completed, the teaching profession came in as one of the five most represented careers in America. Throughout the course of our podcast, we have had millionaire teachers from all over the United States. Yes, we have even had multiple North Carolina Teacher guests who are millionaires as well.

More power to you if you can win the lottery, but these millionaire teachers did not win the lottery. They live below their means, drive cars for 10+ years, don't sell their homes to purchase more expensive homes, invest early, avoid debt, and practice patience.

This isn't some get-rich-quick scheme. This happens slowly over the course of time."

Be Frugal, Be Fearless, and Be a Lifelong Learner.

Made in the USA
Las Vegas, NV
21 January 2024

84692945R00079